Business Communication

Business Communication

Gordon Lord was formerly Head of Communication Studies, Department of Business Education, Kirby College, Cleveland. He is the author of *Know What I Mean?* and *It's My Business To Know*.

Business Communication

for

Secretarial and Clerical Workers

Gordon A. Lord

Chambers Commerce Series

Published by W & R Chambers Ltd Edinburgh, 1987

British Library Cataloguing in Publication Data

Lord, Gordon
    Business Communication — (Chambers commerce series)
    1.
    I. Title

ISBN

Set by Blackwood Pillans & Wilson Ltd. Edinburgh

Printed in Great Britain by
Richard Clay Ltd, Bungay, Suffolk

To JACK and THELMA
in gratitude and with love

Contents

Chapter 9 'I've Got a Job!'

Preface

I wonder how many people actually *read* prefaces? I suspect not many, and, to be honest, I don't always read them myself! However, for those who are taking the trouble to read this, there are a few things that are worth recording.

First, I hope you will find this book more a friendly chat than a formal lecture. I have deliberately used a conversational style, which I believe is easier to read and understand than are impersonal utterances.

Second, I have tried to picture you readers in a variety of situations and in a variety of countries. I have tried to make plain the problems of communication we all have to cope with. I have written this book with the firm belief that most of our problems and differences are exaggerated by, if not actually caused by, inadequate communication and our inability or unwillingness to see another person's point of view. In other words, I want to convey through these pages that a genuine desire to *understand* people is at least as important as learning 'techniques'.

Third, I hope that this book helps you towards achieving the success you are aiming for—qualifications, a satisfying job, entry to higher education or whatever.

Above all I hope you will find it enjoyable.

G.A.L.

Chapter 1

Listening

One of the most valuable skills that any office worker or potential office worker can learn is the skill of *listening*. It is often assumed that all people with unimpaired hearing listen, but this is not so. We are confusing 'listening' with 'hearing' and there is a great difference between the two, as this chapter will try to explain.

1.1 Listening and Hearing

You will have noticed that many animals prick up their ears when an unusual or unexpected sound reaches them. We take this as a sign that they are listening more carefully than usual. In addition, many animals, especially dogs, tilt their heads at an angle, as though trying to catch the very faintest element of the sound that has caught their attention.

Humans are not like this at all. They give little indication of whether they are listening or not. Their ears certainly do not prick up, nor do they alter the position of their heads. You may be speaking to someone who looks at you steadily with an apparently concentrated expression but is in fact thinking about something quite different. Their mind is miles away, as every teacher or lecturer knows from classroom experience!

Animals hear the noises and sounds of day-to-day life but because they have grown accustomed to them they do not show signs of listening. Unfortunately, because speech is one of the day-to-day sounds to which humans have grown accustomed, we also tend only to hear and not to listen to what is being said. We listen only when we want to!

Interestingly, many students like working with background music. Others prefer to work in silence. Of course, there are always background noises of some sort—passing traffic, police sirens, sounds of roadworks in progress, etc.—but these are not noises to

1

which we are *listening*, we merely *hear* them and can therefore concentrate our minds on the task to be done. Whether a student works to music depends on if he *hears* it or *listens* to it.

For many of us, if the background noises reach a certain level, we find it very difficult to concentrate, and this is particularly the case in a busy office, where other people's conversation, doors banging, telephones ringing and the clatter of typewriters may distract us. Consequently, when dealing with a customer or client or trying to have a telephone conversation, we may only *hear* what is being said, rather than truly *listen*.

Let us take an actual situation, in which one person is trying to communicate with another, and try to analyse the factors that affect the communication.

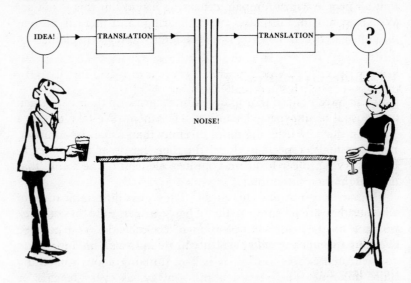

This is a situation in which George and Jane, who are strangers to each other, are occupying opposite ends of a small bar. George wants to strike up a closer acquaintanceship with Jane, and we see that he has an *idea* in his head which he wishes to convey to her.

His first problem is to choose a *medium* through which to communicate. Let us look at some of the possibilities:

Speech
This seems pretty obvious, and is what most of us would choose as our first option.

However, George is faced by certain difficulties, the first of which is that he has to choose which *words* to use in order to be understood. In other words, his first problem is to *translate* his idea into language.

His second problem is: will the language he uses be understood by Jane? He does not know her, so he has no knowledge of what the limits are to her vocabulary; he does not know her background or upbringing; he is unaware of her moral, social, and political background; he does not know her interests, or, to take this to an extreme, whether or not she speaks and understands English!

In other words, he has to *think* very carefully before he speaks.

Then there are Jane's problems. When she *hears* his voice, she hears several words. Her first problem is *translating* them from words into an *idea*. The *meaning* that she puts upon the words may or may not be the same as that George intended to convey. Again, it depends on her education, background, and so on. It also depends on George's, as his choice of words may be unsuitable or misleading. Also, there is the question of whether she is merely hearing or really listening to what George is trying to say, because the extent to which she is really listening will determine (providing his words make sense) how accurately she will receive the idea that is in George's mind.

Writing
Of course, if George had brought a pen with him, and had a beer mat with plenty of space on it, he could use *writing* as a medium for conveying his message. There are still the problems of his *choice of words* and the *translation* of them by Jane. In other words, in addition to the problems above, with the exception of listening, there are *writing* and *reading* skills involved in this method.

Body language
By now you may have thought of other ways George could communicate. For example, simple ideas can be conveyed by facial expressions or gestures, sometimes called *body language,* but the ideas have to be very simple.

Drawings
This is another possibility, but, again, it depends on what the idea is, how good you are at drawing what you want to convey, and how good the receiver is at interpreting the drawing.

Since this chapter is concerned with *listening,* we shall assume that George is going to use *speech* as his medium of communication.

Immediately, he is in trouble. Not only has he the problem of choosing words that express his idea accurately, but also, since he does not have the slightest idea of how they are going to be interpreted, he has to choose simple, understandable words that are not *ambiguous* (that is, capable of more than one meaning).

English is a language in which a large number of words have more than one meaning. For example, many people conclude letters of application for employment with the sentence: 'I hope you will grant me an interview *at your convenience.*' This may well bring a smile to the face of the prospective employer, who may then consign the letter to the bottom of the pile! 'Convenience' means at least two things in English, one of which is lavatory!

George must also *speak clearly* and *loudly* enough to be heard over the background noise.

If you look again at the sketch, you will see three little lines between George's translation of his idea into words and Jane's translation of them back into an idea. These lines represent *noise,* or, to use a more accurate word, *distractions.*

Distractions

We shall consider these under three headings:

Physical distractions

These are the kind mentioned above—outside noises, and the sounds that surround us in a busy work situation. George tries to speak to Jane over the background noise of the bar. She may not be able to hear, let alone listen!

Personal distractions

What we often forget is that not only do our own feelings affect the way we speak but feelings of various kinds also affect the way in which people listen. For instance, it is very difficult to concentrate if you are too hot or too cold, hungry or tired. Pain can seriously interfere with our listening ability, and we all know how having a cold or starting with the flu can make listening to someone very difficult.

George has no idea how Jane is feeling physically. Much of her response will be coloured by these physical feelings, so perhaps, in addition to trying to find the right words and say them clearly, he has to be observant and understand that she may not be feeling at her best. We need the same kind of observation when dealing with clients, customers or colleagues at work, all of whom, if a little bit 'under the weather' may be hearing our replies, questions or comments, but not fully listening to them. Under these circumstances, misunderstandings often arise.

Psychological factors

In addition to our physical state, we also have a number of emotional factors to bear in mind. Sometimes people with whom we try to communicate are under some kind of stress. If, for example, a colleague at work has had some domestic quarrel, or is anxious about the health of a loved one, or is worried by bills that have arrived that morning, the quality of that person's listening will be affected.

Equally, the human mind can easily be distracted by other psychological factors. For instance, we do sometimes become bored in a conversation, talk or lecture, and then the mind begins to wander. Also, it is common that some people, instead of listening to what is being said, are thinking of what they are going to say next! It is no wonder that we hear people saying, 'You didn't listen!' or 'You should have listened more carefully.'

Poor George! With all these things against him, it should come as no surprise if the reply he receives from Jane is not what he hoped for or expected. It should also come as no surprise to us if misunderstandings and mistakes occur at work or at home, or amongst friends socially, when we remember how much concentration is required in order to listen carefully. *Concentration* is a key word in listening, and most of us know this instinctively, which is why we often start a conversation by saying, '*Listen!. . .*'

To *listen* we also need a *motive,* as well as concentration.

Many students are motivated to listen during lectures because they realise that their examination results and probably their future careers depend on getting all the information they can. Soldiers may be motivated to listen to instructors, especially in wartime, as they realise that their lives may depend on what they learn. People tend to listen to doctors and consultants when illness strikes, as they realise that their possible cure may depend on what is being said and what advice is given.

If only we were all as strongly motivated in our daily work, home and social life, we would develop our listening ability and communication would become far more effective.

So far we have examined some of the factors that affect our ability to listen properly. Now let us look at some practical ways in which we can reinforce our listening and make our understanding more thorough.

1.2   Taking Notes

Although many problems are caused by people not listening carefully enough, perhaps an equal number of problems are caused by our faulty or inaccurate *memories*. The human brain has often been likened to a computer or word-processor. Theoretically we all possess a memory bank in which information is stored to be recalled when we need it. However, unlike an electronic machine with a memory, the human recall mechanism is not very efficient. We tend not to be able to remember details, though at the time we receive them we are sure we will remember them. Take telephone numbers, for example—'I am sure to remember that', we think, only to discover later that either we have become unsure of the order of the numbers or we cannot remember them at all. The obvious answer to this problem is to make a note of the number, which can later be transferred to some more permanent storage place, such as a telephone number/address book.

Most of us do not give this procedure a second thought, but realise it is the most practical and commonsense way of assembling a reference book of addresses and telephone numbers. Nevertheless we have a strong reluctance to follow the same method when attending lectures or meetings, when taking instructions (either face-to-face or on the telephone), or when receiving information in situations such as Job Centres, Travel Bureaux, bus or train information desks, and so on. Somehow or other we imagine that not only will we remember the details, but that it is a tedious task to write things down.

Note-taking is therefore one of those tasks that we try to avoid, until we have grasped the idea that not only can we not rely on remembering, but that, unless we have the opportunity to check back with our source of information, we shall be without the details we started out to acquire.

Notes and memos are essential memory aids in the workplace; but to illustrate their importance let us first examine how they contribute to the learning process in the college environment.

Equipment
Every student should be prepared to take notes. Do not imagine that everything will be provided on hand-outs previously prepared

and printed for you. Similarly, you should not rely on notes being dictated, or on that most doubtful of methods, borrowing notes from friends. (You may find with a shock that your friends are relying on notes that *you* have taken!)

The first piece of equipment you need is, rather strangely, something you cannot see or touch. It is *self-discipline*. This means having the will power to carry on with a task once you have started it, and not being put off when you discover difficulties you had not anticipated. Self-discipline is something that cannot be bought at a shop, but unless you have it no amount of equipment will be of any use.

Assuming, then, that you are determined to get down the information you require, the next thing to acquire is a *shorthand-type note pad*. Students so often carry great files into the classroom or lecture theatre unnecessarily. A shorthand notebook, however, is not only easy to carry about; it can also be used for all the subjects on a course, and does not need to be indexed or stored once it is finished with.

The next requirement is an *A4 size ring binder* with an appropriate supply of *A4 paper*.

Since most students will be involved with several subjects or modules, and may have three, four or even five lectures a day, it is also useful to have a set of *dividers* to separate the sets of notes. These can be made quite easily from a relatively cheap pack of coloured cards (A4 size) which will provide easy reference. A useful piece of equipment is an inexpensive *paper punch*, which will provide the holes required for filing information in each section, and for the dividers.

Continuous note-taking throughout lessons or lectures demands self-discipline; so too does the subsequent transfer of the rough jottings in the notebook to an orderly file. However, if you find this transfer of notes a particularly boring chore, remember it is necessary to create a clear and permanent record, both for revision and for reference in the early years of your career. Furthermore this writing-up of notes has a very important learning value.

The learning process

We may take in information during a lecture and understand it, but our *memory* of it is very short—in fact often less than a day. Consequently, at the end of a week we may begin to feel anxious because we have been given so much information and we can remember very little of it, even though we may have made notes in our shorthand notebook quite conscientiously.

However, if we transfer the rough notes into the A4 file *within 24–48 hours* this has the effect of consolidating the information in our minds. To make this more permanent, ideally we should refer to the file about a week later and read through the notes carefully. Often this will fix them in our minds almost permanently. The three charts on page 9 show the nature of what may be called the *learning curve*.

Obviously, if you follow this kind of technique, even if it is demanding, you will gain a much better grasp of your subjects of study, and furthermore you will find revision prior to examinations easier and more reassuring. One of the main reasons why students do not do well in examinations is that they rely too much on remembering what has been heard in lectures, rather than taking the trouble to have adequate notes by the end of the course.

Even when an end-of-course examination is replaced by a continuous assessment system (which is becoming more common these days) the possession of an adequate set of notes is immensely valuable. Remember, also, that after preparation in school or college you hope to be employed. A set of notes to which you can refer if in any doubt will be very helpful in your first job.

Pages 10 and 11 show what a set of lecture notes may look like in your shorthand notebook and what the same notes may look like in your A4 file for future reference.

The 'know-how' of note-taking

There can be no set rules about what should actually be noted during a lecture but there are certain guidelines that may be helpful.

(a) Do not try to note *everything* that is said. If you do you will fall behind the teacher or lecturer, lose heart and probably stop trying to take notes.

(b) Try to pick out the *main points*—ignore illustrations, examples, and other non-essential items.

(c) Note any books to which you may be referred and any information such as statistics, figures, relevant names or other sources of information about the subject.

(d) Do not be afraid to *ask* if anything is not clear, or you think you have missed something of importance.

(e) Use underlining to give emphasis to any item you think might be of special importance or significance.

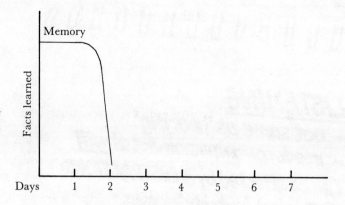

Transferred to file within 2 days

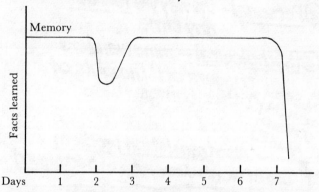

Result of revision after 7 days

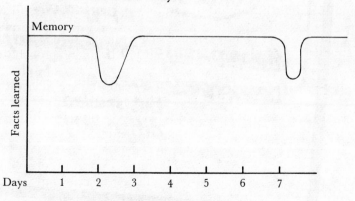

LISTENING
- not same as 'hearing'
- needs CONCENTRATION-act of <u>will</u>

Can be affected by 3 DISTRACTIONS:

① Physical - 'outside' noises

② Personal - the way we <u>feel at</u>
                          any time

③ Psychological - mind wanders
                  'triggers off' thoughts of
WORDS   other things
WHICH
SOUND
ALIKE

Also <u>translation</u> problem
use of words - knowledge of <u>background</u>

of listener   a. family
of speaker   b. education
                c. prejudices

(<u>Malapropisms</u> = wrong words used)

(<u>Homophones</u> = sound alike but
                   but spelled
                   differently)

LISTENING

- not the same as 'hearing' ie not really paying attention

- listening requires CONCENTRATION and is an act of WILL

AFFECTED BY THREE kinds of DISTRACTION:

1 Noises going on round about - especially affecting listening on
   telephone

2 The FEELINGS within the speaker and listener eg pain, temperature,
   tiredness etc

3 Wandering of the mind unless concentrating - 'trigger words' can
   set us thinking of other things, especially words which sound alike
   eg 'let us' and 'lettuce'

(Note: words SOUNDING alike but spelled differently are called HOMOPHONES)

Above distractions grouped as (1) PHYSICAL (2) PERSONAL (3) PSYCHOLOGICAL

When we LISTEN we also have to TRANSLATE words into IDEAS. Ideally, we
should know background (family, education etc) of SPEAKER and realise
our own limitations.

(Note: some people use 'WRONG' words eg 'insistent' for 'assistant' -
these known as MALAPROPISMS)

(f) Do not worry about keeping a neat and tidy shorthand
     notebook. If you write up the notes later, you have the
     opportunity to sort out the information into a clear and
     logical order while it is still fresh in your memory. Notebook
     notes are simply an aid to your memory of the day's (or
     previous day's) lectures; it is the A4 file notes which you are
     going to keep.

The above guidelines apply of course, to any kind of notes you
have to take, whether they are of a telephone conversation, a
meeting, a briefing session at work or any other situation where
you need to have a record of details, procedures or plans for the
future.

Most importantly, these points suppose that you are really
listening to what is being said. If you are merely hearing or thinking
about something else, any serious attempt to take notes will be
doomed to failure.

1.3 Listening to Customers and Clients

Perhaps the best way of beginning this section is to remind
ourselves of the way we put customers, clients or colleagues into
categories. In other words, we tend to pigeon-hole individuals into

either the goods they want, the complaints they may wish to make, or the jobs that they do.

I wonder if we are dehumanising the people whom we label in this way? We refer to one as 'a buyer', to another as 'a complainant', and to our colleagues as 'the secretary', 'the telephonist' or 'the office junior'. Often we lose sight of the fact that *they are people,* with feelings and individual peculiarities. This may very well affect the way we *listen* to them. Unless we remember that everything they say is to some extent affected by their feelings and personal make-up, we may respond less helpfully and with less understanding than should be the case.

Perhaps many customers and clients can present their needs reasonably clearly, but there are also many 'awkward' customers who waste a lot of time (or so it seems to you) talking about themselves, about unnecessary details, about anything or everything except the purchase or business in hand. Under these circumstances we tend to react in various ways: we may become impatient, even short-tempered and abrupt; we may become bored and simply stop listening; we may even become angry and aggressive. These reactions are likely to lose us a customer or client.

Similarly, misunderstandings and conflict with our colleagues can arise because we lack the patience, understanding or tolerance to listen to them carefully. Again this sort of breakdown in communication is the result of a failure in attention; of merely hearing instead of *listening*. We so often forget that customers, clients and colleagues are liable to suffer the same kind of variation of feelings that we do.

What all this means is that much of our communication, especially in speech, is coloured and often marred by *personal feelings*. If our feelings affect our *listening,* this will affect our understanding of another person's needs and, in turn, the nature of our response to them.

Once we recognise this fact, we should be able to listen to customers, clients, and colleagues with an awareness of both *their* feelings and *our own*. If, for example, you have to deal with a customer and you have a headache, you can tell yourself, 'I have a bit of a headache. I need to listen even more carefully or my headache will simply make me want to get rid of the customer as soon as possible. I may say the first thing that comes into my head without thinking carefully about my answers and I may therefore confuse or mislead the customer just to get rid of him or her.'

Prejudice and bias

It is worth at this point considering the mental attitudes that we all have, and how they too may affect the quality of our listening. The *thoughts* and *beliefs* that we developed throughout our childhood, and perhaps are not even consciously aware of having, influence our interpretation of what we hear and what we say.

We all put *our own* meanings and interpretations on to what people say. When we speak to others, we are speaking from a point of view (or a position of prejudice and bias) that they may not have, and therefore we are misunderstood, just as we misunderstand them.

We can perhaps understand this more clearly if we look at a few examples.

1 How many of us do reasonably well in some subjects at school and have one in which we do badly? When we analyse the reason why, usually we admit we disliked the teacher of that subject! Perhaps we felt that the teacher treated us badly, unfairly, and always gave preference to his or her 'favourites'. Whatever the reason, we disliked the teacher and therefore *we did not listen*.

2 You do not have to work for long in some firms before you discover that everything the management suggest is treated with the greatest *suspicion*. 'What are they after? What's in it for us? It's just a way of getting more work out of us for less money!' are the kind of comments heard. Before long you can acquire the same prejudiced attitude, and greet every suggestion with suspicion.

3 If you have ever worked in a shop, how have you felt when you have been approached by an unshaven, ill-kempt character? Have you really *listened* to what he is trying to say? Or have you been so prejudiced by his appearance and mannerisms that you have not even tried to understand?

4 Whatever religion you have, have you ever attended a place of worship of a different faith, in order to try and understand their beliefs? If you are interested in politics, have you ever taken the trouble to attend the meeting of a party other than your own or read newspaper articles expressing a different point of view from your own?

There are many more examples of the way that we become isolated and *insulated* by our prejudices and beliefs, erecting barriers against anyone different from ourselves, until we are incapable of really *listening* to what they have to say.

This last section on listening is really about *listening impartially,* that is, without prejudice, without fear, without letting our own feelings get in the way of the flow of communication. Only in this way can we learn to *listen with understanding,* and though it may not be easy, this is utterly worthwhile!

Questions

1 Describe in about ten lines what you understand as the difference between hearing and listening.
2 Name the three basic 'distractions' that interfere with listening. Give an example of each, other than those given in this book.
3 A friend of yours is about to start a college course. Write a short letter to him or her about the value of taking notes and how to set about it.

Chapter 2

Speaking

The purpose of this chapter is to consider some of the problems created by *speech*, and some of the ways in which we can deal with these problems. Speech is so fundamental to our dealings with other people that we tend to forget it is a skill, which, like any other skill, must be worked at if we are to communicate more effectively.

It is true that as babies we pick up the rudiments of speech with little apparent effort. However, some people never go very far beyond the limited and 'natural' stage of speech picked up as a child, and consequently are very restricted when trying to express ideas beyond the simplest level. Unless these limitations are tackled, helped by reading, listening to more able speakers, finding out what words mean, and so on, they will be a barrier for the rest of one's life.

2.1 Factors that Affect Speech

Let us look at some of the influences that affect our speech.

Accent

As a baby grows older, he is influenced not only by the words spoken around him, but also by the *accent* in which they are spoken. If a child grows up in a family and community where the local accent is strong the chances are he will speak that way too. He knows no other. Of course, television can be a strong influence on speech, but even there, especially in children's programmes, presenters speak with quite strong local accents. Many school-teachers have strong local accents, so how could a child learn to speak without one?

This raises the obvious question: What is wrong with having a strong local accent, anyway? The answer is *nothing*! Most accents are interesting, colourful, and give character to what is being said.

15

However, there are some situations in life where they are out of place and become a hindrance, a barrier to communication. This is particularly the case in business and commerce, especially when you have to deal with people from other parts of your country and from other countries too.

If you spend most of your life in one particular area and work in any kind of job where you do not have to deal with the public and where you do not have to telephone people in different parts of your country, your local accent will be no particular drawback. However, a strong local accent may be a handicap if you wish to work in another part of your country—you may find difficulty getting employment outside your home region as your accent goes against you at interviews. Similarly, if you deal with members of the public you may have a problem making yourself understood, particularly to clients or customers from other areas or countries.

Dialect

Closely associated with accent, but not the same thing at all, is *dialect*.

Different areas, even different towns and villages in the same area, have developed over the years different languages. In Britain, the foundation of them all is English, of course, but words have been added or changed from their original form so that often only the local inhabitants understand what is being said. Without going into how and why these changes have taken place, we have to recognise that if we are brought up in a particular area, the chances are that we inherit many of these different words and sometimes may use them without realising that to anyone from another area they are incomprehensible. Since these words and phrases are often combined with the local accent they become even more difficult to understand.

The use of dialect words phrased in the local accent is called speaking in *the vernacular,* or *patois* or *argot*. This happens in nearly every country, and in some cases people from adjacent villages cannot understand each other at all.

Colloquialisms

Yet another stumbling-block in our attempts to communicate in speech is our often unconscious use of *colloquialisms*. If dialect is the use of local words and phrases that differ from standard English, then colloquialisms are *local speech patterns*—that is, it is the arrangement of the words that is unfamiliar, or confusing to the outsider. Colloquialisms can be described as everyday speech, informal and unsophisticated—the kind we use to friends and family, but which differs from area to area.

If a person from Tyneside in the North of England tells you to 'Gan canny, man!' he is telling you to 'go carefully', but is using both dialect and accent. The only bit of colloquial speech is in the addition of the word 'man'. In Wales, they may say 'Go carefully, boyo' or 'Go carefully, look you'. On the other hand, if you talk to someone from the Teesside area of England he (or she) may ask you what you do *on a night*. Many people from other parts of Britain may not understand this, as they would say 'during the evening'; 'on a night' is a colloquialism.

Lack of adequate vocabulary
People do not always know the right words to use when trying to communicate, so they make do with words that approximate what they intend to say.

One of the major causes of this is the use we make of 'lazy' words: words that do not describe our meaning accurately or precisely, but which suggest vaguely what we intend to say. Such words are 'good', 'nice', 'bad' and many others. You have only to listen to someone talking about their holiday to hear such sentences as 'Yes, we had a *nice* time, the weather was *nice,* the food in the hotel was quite *nice* and the people we met were *nice* too. It was a *nice* journey, but it's *nice* to be back home again!' Now what exactly does the speaker try to say? 'We had an *enjoyable* time, the weather was *sunny* and *fine,* the food in the hotel was *well cooked* and excellently *presented,* and the people we met were *very pleasant* and *companionable.* The journey was *comfortable,* but I am *happy* to be home again!' (Perhaps you can think of other words the speaker may have used to replace the word *nice.*)

Malapropisms
Mistakes made by using wrong or inappropriate words are called *malapropisms*; for example, 'he was not illegible to take the examination'. In this case 'illegible' has been used instead of 'eligible'.

Laziness in speech
This can take several forms. For example:
  (a) Failure to give correct names to things or people, for example, 'Pass me the thingy on the whatsit, will you?'

(b) Lazy pronunciation, for example, 'Gerroff me desk! Y'll muck up everythin'.' This sounds a little bit like accent or dialect, but lazy speech is found in all areas, dialects, and accents.

(c) Failure to *think* before speaking, for example, 'Er, well, it was, er, you know, like kind of, er, you know what I mean. . .'

(d) Failure to *pronounce* words clearly, e.g. When someone on the telephone says 'This is a bad line, will you speak up, please' he usually means, 'For heaven's sake speak more clearly; you're mumbling!'

Ambiguity

There are two main sources of ambiguity:

1   the use of a word or phrase that may mean more than one thing,

2   the use of what in textbooks is called the 'misrelated participle'.

1   A word or phrase can easily be construed or interpreted in more than one way. We have already seen the ambiguous use of 'convenience'. Take the following extract from a newspaper as another example:

> The Mayor and members of the Council
> took the collection, *while* the Bishop of X
> preached the sermon.

Notice that the use of the word *while* is misleading. Does it mean *and* or does it mean *during the time that*—surely not the latter! Of course, common sense may tell you what the writer *means* to say, but misunderstandings can easily arise.

2   The misrelated participle error often happens because writers or speakers are unaware of its existence. It happens most frequently when we begin a sentence with a present participle. The present participle is that part of a verb or action word that ends in '-ing', such as 'having', 'being', or 'going'. Once we *start* a sentence with such a word, we must be very careful to state the person or thing *doing the action* as soon as possible, otherwise we create an ambiguous statement. For example, we may say or write, 'Cycling through the park, a dog bit me!' Even if we start with the

words 'whilst cycling . . .' it still sounds as though the *dog* was doing the cycling.

The cause of this ambiguity is that the *subject* of the sentence (i.e. the person or thing doing the action) is placed at the end of the sentence, instead of being closely associated with the participle. If the sentence had been expressed as 'Whilst I was cycling . . .' or 'Cycling through the park, I was bitten by a dog' this ambiguity would have been avoided.

This kind of ambiguity is very common—even in business correspondence. One reads, for example, a letter that says: 'Having taken your cheque to the bank this morning, the manager refused to cash it'. Does the writer mean that the manager took the cheque to the bank? Common sense tells us that he or she does not, but why should the reader or listener have to work out the meaning? So *be careful* if you wish to start a sentence with a participle!

Errors in sentence construction

These are many, but the worst of them has already been referred to as *ambiguity*. Another common error we commit is in the placing of *adverbs* in a sentence. An adverb qualifies, modifies or changes in some way the meaning of a verb, adjective, preposition, conjunction or another adverb. It can affect every part of speech except a noun or pronoun. We might, for example, refer to the 'fat man'. If we used the phrase '*very* fat man' we should be using an adverb to qualify the adjective 'fat'.

Unfortunately there are some adverbs, especially the word 'only', which can easily be put in the wrong place and thus distort the *meaning* of the sentence. Look at the following:

> *Only* he owed me five pounds.
> He *only* owed me five pounds.
> He owed *only* me five pounds.
> He owed me *only* five pounds.

You will see that there are four different meanings in the above sentences. Which does the writer or speaker really mean? There is no way of knowing for sure.

It is common to hear the weather forecaster on television say: 'the temperature tonight will only rise to 5 degrees'. What are we to gather from this? That it will not fall, and that it can only go up?

Or do they really mean that 'the temperature will rise to *only* 5 degrees'?

The difference between *saying* and *meaning* is quite considerable. (And incidentally, the use of the adverb 'quite' is often careless, as we frequently use it to mean 'fairly' or 'almost' when in fact it means 'definitely'!)

Jargon and commercialese

You will probably find that in most textbooks on Business English, jargon is condemned as thoroughly undesirable and in its generally understood sense it is wise to avoid it. Jargon means the use of language that only those 'in the know' will understand. By jargon we usually mean that to the average person who has no specialised knowledge of a subject or work situation, the words and phrases used convey nothing.

Commercialese, on the other hand, is the use of old-fashioned business phrases, such as 'inst.', 'prox.' and 'ult.' for 'this month', 'next month' and 'last month'. This has almost died out.

If you work in an office the chances are that you will quickly pick up words and phrases that people 'outside' will not understand. But every educational subject has its jargon; every sport, every field of human activity, has its specialised words and phrases, and between people who understand them these are time-saving. The danger lies in assuming that people outside that particular activity will also understand them.

'Ah,' we might say to the little old lady standing at the counter, 'what you need is an X3/752, but if Section 7 doesn't apply, an X3/757 – unless you're a pensioner, of course, and in that case it's a OAP/X/753. Now it depends on what collateral you can put up, of course . . . .' By this time our client is very confused!

2.2   Speaking to Customers and Clients

Once you are aware that careless language can be an obstruction to communication, you can get to work on the task of expressing yourself clearly and directly.

However, do not forget to be sensitive to the needs of your listeners. There is one use of jargon that is quite commendable. 'To learn the native jargon' means to take the trouble to communicate with people on their own terms. Whenever we meet someone who needs a careful and helpful explanation we should adapt our language to *their* understanding or 'start from where they are'. We do this instinctively when we talk to children. This is not the same as 'talking down to people' or 'being condescending'; it is simply showing a genuine desire to understand and be understood.

When we communicate with people for whom English is a second language we need to take special care and use words and phrases that are likely to be familiar to the listener.

Never make assumptions on the basis of age or dress when communicating with people. Accents may also be misleading, and speed of speech is not an indicator of the deftness of thought.

2.3 Speaking on the Telephone

It may seem strange to include a section on speaking on the telephone, as for most of us telephoning, either receiving or making calls, is something to which we have become very accustomed. However, the telephoning that takes place in a busy office is rather different to the casual calls we receive and make at home.

Be prepared!

First, you should always have a pen and paper by an office telephone; avoid having to ask a caller to 'hold on a minute' until you fetch a piece of paper and a pencil.

Skills

There are several skills involved in receiving telephone calls from clients or customers, or from other business organisations.

(a) We must be able to 'take notes', as we discussed earlier. Communication within an organisation depends frequently on a person's ability to receive fairly detailed and complicated messages, and it is essential that the information we have to pass on should be accurate and complete. Never rely on your memory!

(b) It is very important to be sure that any numbers, addresses, names, or information of a similar nature should be correct. Therefore we should always read back the information to the caller to check that it is right. It is so easy to confuse a reference or account number that we need to be absolutely sure it is correct. Names can also be confusing, so a caller should be asked to spell the name, and the address if there is one, to avoid error.

(c) Above all, there is the problem of speech. We have already considered the problems created by accent, colloquialisms, dialect words and phrases and so on. If your caller has a strong accent—and it may not be one you are familiar with—you should listen very carefully, and ask the caller to repeat information if you are not quite sure what has been said. Any phrases you do not understand should be explained at your request, and of course, any replies you give have also to be understandable to the caller, which is another reason why you should try to speak as clearly as possible, and why you should choose your words carefully.

(d) Sometimes the telephone line may not be a good one. If this is the case, tell the caller and offer to ring him or her back; it may be that you get a better line. So often mistakes are caused by a poor connection that distorts words and causes you to record the wrong information, or to be misunderstood by the caller.

(e) Finally, every message you record that has to be passed on should be written out clearly and legibly and given immediately to the person for whom it is intended; even if it does not *seem* to be important.

Much of the above is simply common sense, of course, but neglect of these points causes the breakdown of communication in an office, which every member of staff should try to avoid.

This 'telephone technique' is really a matter of *habit*. Once you get into the routine of dealing with telephone calls in this way you will just do it automatically, and the organisation will be the better for it.

2.4 Giving Oral Reports

It is unlikely that you will be asked to submit written reports soon after you first start work, though knowing how to do them will be to your advantage if you wish to apply for a promotion. In a senior position you will almost certainly be required to write reports.

It is more than likely, however, that soon after starting work you will have to give an *oral* or *verbal* report (i.e. by word of mouth) to a senior. There is no need to worry about this providing you know how to set about presenting a written report. This is dealt with in Section 6.3.

The following guidelines will help you not only to present a good report but also to reduce anxiety:

(a) The first step is to *prepare* well and to remember the pattern of the *informal* report as a starting point (see p. 77). It consists of two sections—the first giving the *facts* and the second giving *opinions* and possibly *suggestions*.

(b) Make notes on paper (about postcard size), to hold in one hand. Do not be tempted to write out the report in full. The notes are simply a memory aid to keep you on track.

(c) If you are interrupted by a question, so disturbing your flow of thought and ideas, place a finger immediately on the place in the notes at which the interruption took place.

Once you have answered the question, (even though you may simply have to reply, 'I'm sorry, but I don't know') you can then return to where you were in the notes without difficulty.

(d) The report should be given *clearly*—that means special attention to *pronunciation* and the *speed* of speaking. It is always better to try and speak *more slowly* than in normal conversation.

(e) Try to *look* at the person to whom you are talking, even though from time to time you may have to glance down at your notes. It is irritating to a listener if the speaker is talking to the ceiling or the floor!

(f) If you feel a bit nervous, in spite of being well prepared, it may help if you take some deep breaths before starting

Much of what is written here and in the following section is also useful advice when going for an *interview*; we shall be looking at this in more detail in Chapter 9.

2.5 Speaking in Public

Most of us can talk quite happily to a friend or colleague at work; we can chat calmly with a group of people at home or out in an informal setting, but let someone ask us to speak to a group on a special occasion or to a class in college, and we may well start to quiver like the proverbial jelly, and to feel that the end of the world has just been announced! It is small consolation to be told that nearly everyone reacts in this way when asked to speak in public, but it may be more surprising to learn that even very experienced speakers have similar qualms.

Overcoming nerves
The first thing to remember when speaking in public is that most of the audience will be sympathetic and will understand the ordeal you are going through.

They will not want to watch you make a fool of yourself, or to criticise, or to catch you out making mistakes; and they certainly will feel embarrassed for you if you show signs of stress and anxiety. They will listen courteously until you have finished and will understand something of what you may have been feeling before you began.

Preparation

The next point to remember is the importance of *being prepared*. Only very experienced speakers will speak *ex tempore* (without preparation) and then they are probably speaking on a subject that they know very well, and for which they *did* prepare once, however long ago.

All really effective speakers *know what they want to say* and everything they say leads to *one clear idea*. However, preparation not only means knowing *what* you want to say but *how* you want to say it. This means putting your ideas *in order*, then finding suitable examples and illustrations to make the points clear.

If you want to write out your talk in full, by all means do so, but it would be wise to reduce it finally to a set of notes, because you should *never read* a talk or address. Reading a script sounds unnatural, unless you are an experienced actor. Learn it 'off by heart' if you must, but better still just have a short set of notes, preferably on postcard-size cards or paper, to remind you of the flow of ideas. It does not always settle the nerves to memorise a speech because there is always the fear that you might forget your lines, so try to use notes and to think on your feet. You will find that after a few rehearsals you will be able to cope quite well, though you may never say exactly the same thing twice!

Breathing

Breathing properly is a great help when speaking in public. If you take too deep a breath your words will tend to come out in a rush; if you do not take in sufficient breath your voice will fade away before you get to the end of the sentence.

Only practice will help you to learn how much breath you need to maintain a steady and *audible* flow of speech, remembering that you have to speak *more slowly* than normally and *loudly enough* to reach the people who are at the back.

However, it is a good thing to take a deep breath or two *before* you begin, as this tends to 'steady you down'. This is also useful to remember when going in for an interview or when giving a report.

Often the audience will be strangers to you and you will be unable to predict their response. However, when you first begin speaking in public you usually know many if not all of your audience, and this can help you decide how to deliver what you have to say.

For example, if your listeners are known to you, you may decide to introduce a joke or two. This may be alright if you can tell a funny story effectively, but it is a disaster if you cannot. It is best *not* to use a humorous approach unless you are sure you can do it well. Other kinds of story—personal anecdotes and so on—can be quite effective if not too long-winded or dull. In general, it is wise to remember the *advice to public speakers*: 'Stand up. Speak up. Then shut up.'

If you have taken note of the suggestions above, you will find that there is no need to feel unduly anxious about speaking in public, though it is natural to feel a certain amount of tension before you begin. If you have prepared well, tried to anticipate your audience, and practised speaking loudly, clearly, and slowly, just remember that the audience is on your side!

Once you have accepted the challenge of speaking to a group, you will find it is not as frightening as you thought; and when you have done it a few times you will have a definite advantage if you wish to apply for a more responsible post at work. Any applicant who can speak reasonably well to a group or at an interview has an advantage over others who cannot.

Speech is such a basic element in communication that it is rather sad and a little depressing to realise how little attention we give to it. One of the best ways of learning this skill or art, if you are not lucky enough to have been born with a pleasant voice, is to listen to yourself over and over again on a tape recorder and to *practise* adjusting the pitch of your voice until you have achieved a reasonable sound.

2.6 The Way We Speak to Others

Up to now we have been considering what might be called the mechanics of speech, but no chapter on speaking would be complete without reference to the *manner* and *tone of delivery* of what we have to say. Speaking clearly, loudly and slowly enough are important, but so too is the *tone of voice* we use when we address others.

Speech can be a very powerful tool, and we can do a great deal of good or a great deal of harm by our use of it.

Up to now we have been considering ways of improving our powers of speech, but we must also remember that it is not only a matter of how good we are at speaking, but also *to what use* we put this ability.

For example, our speech can be helpful, informative and constructive when we deal with others; it can also be hurtful, emotionally disturbing and destructive.

Sarcasm

Perhaps the first and most powerfully destructive weapon in the armoury of speech is *sarcasm*. Sarcasm aims to *diminish* or *belittle* someone, especially in the presence of others, and is a nasty and hurtful way of upsetting someone.

Most of us have suffered from the use of sarcasm by others against us. Some school-teachers use it; some parents use it; some colleagues at work use it; sometimes our so-called friends use it. Nevertheless one should avoid it: it usually arouses resentment and antagonism and can only worsen a relationship.

Innuendo

A much gentler and more effective way of speaking can be achieved through the use of *innuendo*. Unlike sarcasm this is simply 'dropping a hint' or saying something from which the listener is supposed to draw his or her own conclusions. Of course, this can also be damaging and hurtful.

Perhaps a couple of examples will show the difference between these two ways of speaking:

(a) The supervisor throws down a letter on a typist's desk and says, loudly enough for all the office to hear: 'Anybody would think you'd typed this with your feet! You're not paid for your brilliant incompetence, you know!' This is sarcasm—openly hurtful and belittling.

(b) The same situation, but this time the supervisor says: 'Look – you *did* get a Grade I Pass in typing didn't you? I'm sure you can improve on this.' This is innuendo and, if accompanied by a smile and a gentle tone, is likely to be much less hurtful and to cause little resentment.

We should *never* speak without regard to the other person's feelings. The best advice is probably not to use either sarcasm or innuendo to make a point. It is just as easy, if someone needs to be corrected, to say: 'Don't you think it would be better if . . .' or, 'Can you suggest any way we might improve. . . .' After all, the purpose of speech is *to communicate*, not to set up barriers of resentment and antagonism.

Try to keep this in mind whenever you talk to *anyone*. Of course, not everyone will speak to *you* in this positive way—but that's their problem, not yours!

Questions

1 Think about the way you speak, then make a list of the *changes* you think you could and should make to improve your speech. (Be honest—even if it hurts!)
2 English has many *homophones*–words that sound the same but are spelled differently and have different meanings. Write down at least twenty words which sound the same but have different meanings, e.g. bear/bare, pair/pear/pare. Then write a short sentence using both or all the words to show their different meanings, for instance: The sight of the *bare* and starving prisoners was more than she could *bear*. I *pared* a *pair* of *pears*.
3 Prepare a short address or speech to last about three minutes on one of the following subjects:
   (a) The problems of speaking on the telephone in an office.
   (b) How you would speak to a customer who (i) is very nervous and stammers, (ii) does not speak English very well, (iii) is angry and aggressive. (Your talk should be in three parts, each dealing with (i), (ii), and (iii) above.)
4 'People may mean what they say, but they don't often say what they mean.' Write a brief comment on this statement, and give two or three examples of the weaknesses in speech or writing that may lead to misunderstanding.
5 What is the present participle and what is the rule we should follow to avoid ambiguity when starting a sentence with one?
6 You have been asked to attend a staff meeting where you have to give an *oral* report on the condition of the fire extinguishers in your office.

   Draw up a set of notes you might use for this report. (If you do not work in an office, it will be useful to find out the information you require from an inspection of your school or college department and consult with the appointed fire officer or safety committee.)

Chapter 3

Reading

When, in Alice in Wonderland, Alice asked the Mock Turtle what he was taught at school, she was at first puzzled by the reply, 'Reeling and Writhing, of course!', until she realised that what the speaker meant was '*Reading* and *Writing*'!

Reading is the sort of skill we have acquired to a fairly competent level by the time we leave school. Unfortunately, because we can read newspapers, magazines and record sleeves with little trouble, we seldom bother to tackle anything demanding greater concentration. In fact, to suggest to some people that they pick up a book and actually *read* it is enough to make them reel!

The importance of reading both to the student and the office worker, cannot be overstressed. Just as the student should know how and where to gather information, and should not be intimidated by hefty volumes, the office worker should be able to deal confidently and efficiently with any documents, forms or other papers she may be called upon to handle. Consequently this chapter is designed to highlight ways in which you can develop your reading skills.

3.1 Different Reading Skills

It may come as a surprise to some to learn that there are at least three different 'skills' or 'levels' as far as reading is concerned.

First, there is the skill we acquire at school, which usually enables us to read magazines, newspapers, and the simpler type of book without much trouble. This might be called 'normal' reading and is the only level many people acquire.

Second, the student or office worker who requires summaries of various documents, or who needs to seek particular information in a variety of books or papers has to be able to read very rapidly. Our normal reading speed is approximately 250 words a minute; the

28

speed required for rapid reading or 'skimming' is up to 1000 words a minute.

Third, if you want to study for some professional or technical qualification, you quickly find that the 'normal' kind of reading is really inadequate. You encounter problems with vocabulary, for one thing, and also difficulties in understanding complex ideas and arguments. At this academic level you have to be able to read *critically* and to make comparisons with other writers' ideas. You need the ability to read *in depth*.

Perhaps by now you will have realised that there is a lot more to reading than meets the eye.

Normal reading

First, then, you should develop your *normal* reading skill.

Reading thoughtfully is the way to begin. This means trying to understand more fully what the writer is trying to say.

Reading more widely is essential in order to increase your vocabulary and to experience a wider variety of writing styles and techniques.

Reading critically enables you to compare one writer's style with another's, to compare one writer's ideas with another's, and to assess the appropriateness of grammatical constructions, vocabulary and tone.

Skim reading

This is a familiar word to most people. It means 'to travel quickly over the surface', and this can be applied to a type of reading.

As already stated, there are many occasions when we need to 'glance through' written matter as we seek some particular piece of information. This may involve using several publications and the most important element is *speed*.

Speed reading requires considerable practice, but after a few weeks we should be able to increase our speed of reading to four times what it was, if we know the technique to use.

Actually, we have to return to a method that we used when first learning to read. Perhaps you remember the days when you placed your finger under a word and tried laboriously to put the letters together. The same technique is now used for speed reading. This time you place your finger under each line and move it rapidly along. With practice, you will be surprised at the way in which information can be gained very rapidly, and a further refinement, when you have become proficient in moving the finger along the

line, is to run the finger *down* the page and still be able to take in the
gist of what is written there.

Of course, you cannot take in the technical or specialist detail,
but you can grasp enough of the meaning to know whether you
have reached the passage you were looking for.

Depth reading

This is the opposite of speed reading and at the beginning is often
painfully slow and demanding. Yet it is essential for all people
handling textbooks or complex publications, such as new legisla-
tion made by Parliament, policy statements and scientific reports.

The main purpose of this kind of reading is to improve our
knowledge and understanding of what we are reading, and to enable us
to grasp quite difficult and complex arguments. In order to do this
effectively we first need self discipline.

For example, every time you come across a word that is strange
or unfamiliar you must (a) look up the *general* meaning in the
dictionary, (b) note the *different* meanings if there are two or more,
and (c) decide which of the meanings the writer intends us to
understand in the particular sentence or phrase used. Finally, you
should note the word and its different uses in the 'vocabulary'
section of your notebook.

To take a simple example: suppose you read that 'the detective
found a *solution'*. There is no way of knowing just what the word
'solution' means in this sentence. If you look it up in a dictionary
you find at least two meanings: it may mean the answer to a puzzle
or problem, or it may mean a solid dissolved in a liquid. It seems
likely that the writer means us to put the first meaning to the word,
though if the detective is investigating a crime committed in a
science laboratory it could possibly be the second meaning that is
implied.

Students are sometimes heard to say that at the beginning of a
course of study the things they have to read are *hard*. What they
probably mean is that the material contains a lot of unfamiliar
words and phrases.

Now the whole point about 'reading in depth' is *not to go on
reading* until you are sure about the meaning of a word or phrase.
Although this is hard and slow work at first, it gradually gets easier,
as once you have noted the meaning of a word or phrase it is not
strange the next time you encounter it.

You should make use of comprehensive dictionaries, ency-
clopedias and specialist reference books; and *ask* (teachers,

lecturers or librarians) if you cannot find an answer straightaway. Depth reading gives you the sense of satisfaction that you thoroughly understand a text and that your reading has been worthwhile.

3.2 Library Facilities

Most people know that a library is available if they want to borrow books, but television and videos distract many young people from this service.

Reading books is a very good habit to acquire when one is young—not only because of the wealth of information one can gain but also, and more importantly, because reading is one of the best ways of learning how to handle language and to express ideas. These skills are much less likely to be acquired from watching television. Even light reading for pleasure can help you to grasp the use of language, but the serious student needs also to select those books that broaden their understanding of the subjects being studied on their course.

A modern library offers far more than books, however. It has, for example, video tapes, cassettes, teaching machines, photo-copying facilities and many other aids to learning. A wide range of pamphlets and brochures is available for those who want to know 'What's on' locally in the entertainment line; people wanting to start their own business can find useful information; Citizens Advice Bureau, Legal Aid and Consumer Protection leaflets are also on display; there is a variety of posters and visual material available on local, national and international matters, and enquiries made at the reference section of a library will usually produce information, advice, facts and figures on almost any imaginable topic. A variety of local and national newspapers is also available, and in larger central libraries a selection of foreign newspapers too, together with magazines covering a very wide range of hobbies, interests, professions and trades.

All in all, a library contains a wealth of information on most subjects, and if it does not have a particular piece of requested information the staff will usually manage to obtain it within a day or two, if asked.

The cataloguing system

Perhaps the first thing to become familiar with in the library is the system of cataloguing the books.

It is not a difficult system to use. Usually there are two sets of files—one listing book titles, the other listing books under the names of the authors—and either will tell you where the books you want can be found. A division is made between 'fiction' and 'non-fiction' too, so that access to any book is relatively easy.

Much more could be written about the library and its services; but the best thing to do is to go and see for yourself. Join, if you are not already a member, and set yourself a target of, say, one book a week to begin with, gradually working up to two, three or four a week as your reading progresses.

You will be surprised how your general knowledge and your knowledge and use of English will improve. Furthermore the quality of your own written work should show an appreciable improvement.

3.3   Foreign Phrases Used in English

Although we keep referring to 'English' we have always to remember that the language which we call by that name is really a 'mongrel' language. It has many different ancestors—Celtic, Norse, Danish, Latin, Norman and French—and over the centuries a considerable number of words have been added from all over the world. For example, tulip comes from a pure Turkish word; bungalow is Indian; bazaar is Arabic.

Certain professions, particularly the legal ones, use foreign phrases without an 'English' translation. A judge, for example, may say that he will hear a case *in camera,* or that the matter is *sub judice,* or that the social worker will be *in loco parentis* of a child since the mother is *non compos mentis.*

If you work in a solicitor's office, the chances are that you will fairly quickly learn the meanings of such phrases. However, the rest of us should also know them.

Some of the more common Latin phrases are:
in camera—in secret; privately
ad hoc—for this special purpose
ex officio—by reason of an official position
ex cathedra—officially pronounced
ipso facto—by that fact
per se—by or in itself
bona fides—honest intentions; good faith
locum tenens—deputy or 'stand-in' (usually for a doctor and referred to as a 'locum')
multum in parvo—much in little space

There are many more words and phrases that you should look up in a good dictionary when you meet them.

Also useful to know are Latin *prefixes,* which are attached to the beginning of a word and cause the meaning to be changed. Some common examples are:

    ante—before (antenatal = before birth)
    post—after (postoperative = after the operation)
    pre—before (pre-Christmas shopping = before Christmas)
    sub—under (submarine = under sea)
    super—above, beyond (superficial = on the surface)

Greek words are usually found in scientific and medical vocabularies. Perhaps the most common example is the *suffix* or ending '-ology'. We interpret this as 'the study of', hence ge-(earth)-ology, dermat-(skin)-ology, psych-(mind)-ology.

Useful prefixes to distinguish between are *'hyper-'* and *'hypo-';* the former means 'above or over' (as in 'hypersensitive'); the latter means 'under', as in 'hypodermic' (under the skin).

French has been a great influence on our language for many centuries. The number of French phrases in use is too great to note here. Whenever you hear or read one that is unfamiliar, look it up.

Italian and German terms are particularly associated with music, but we also use some of them in a metaphorical sense (see next section). For example, we use 'presto' (Italian for 'very quickly') when we want someone to 'get a move on'.

Many people question the use of foreign-language phrases in speech and writing, arguing that they are confusing to people who are unfamiliar with them. Others say that these phrases are much more precise than their English equivalents, and therefore defend them. The fact is that they are still in use, and if we come into contact with them, we need to extend our vocabulary to include them.

3.4   Figures of Speech

In addition to its foreign phrases, English is particularly rich in 'figures of speech'. Each of these has a special name to identify it, but unless you are a student of English literature there is little need to learn them. However, there are two principal figures of speech that we do need to recognise. They are the most commonly used, and they can be very confusing if they are not used properly. They are the *metaphor* and the *simile.*

Metaphor

The word itself means 'change of meaning'; every metaphor is intended to mean something different from what the words, taken at their face value, would suggest.

When someone says 'I was so late getting up this morning that I had to *fly*!', you do not suppose for a moment that they really mean it. They are saying only that they had to hurry. In other words, you should not take their words *literally*.

Many of our proverbs and sayings are metaphorical; for instance, when we hear someone referred to as 'a black-hearted villain' we are not supposed to assume that this is the actual colour of the person's heart!

Simile

The other common figure of speech is the *simile*. We use this to compare one thing with another when they have one feature in common but in all other respects are *not* alike. For example, we say someone is 'as bright as a button' or that he 'ran like lightning'. Notice that in these cases, the words 'like' or 'as' appear. We can always identify a simile in this way.

Beware of the dangers of using metaphors and similes inappropriately. While it may be acceptable to include two related metaphors in one sentence, metaphors from unrelated sources should not be juxtaposed. For instance: 'As soon as she knew the ropes she nailed her colours to the mast and told her supervisor how communication within the office could be improved' does not confuse the reader as it makes use of two related nautical metaphors. On the other hand, 'He's a rat, riding roughshod over their feelings like that!' is nonsense, suggesting that the subject is in one moment a rat, and the next a horse.

Similarly metaphors and similes should not be mixed together in the same sentence, and the use of either must be appropriate to the subject under discussion. We should also remember that in some languages there is no such thing as a metaphor, so many people who are not native English speakers can be very confused by English usage.

Similes can be *overworked*. This means that they lose their effectiveness because they have become too familiar. The phrase 'as green as grass' has been so overused that it has become a *cliché*, that is to say that it has ceased to have any effect on the listener or reader.

3.5   Reading Between the Lines

So far this chapter has highlighted the importance of understanding each individual word in a passage if we want to grasp the writer's overall message. However, sometimes, indeed quite often, writers do not 'say what they mean'.

In fact, many writers rely on the reader being able to interpret a meaning that is by no means clear from the words used, and which may even be the very opposite of the words used.

Interpretation or, as it is sometimes called, comprehension, depends on a number of skills and abilities possessed by the reader.

Use of words
The first skill required is a knowledge of vocabulary.

Once we begin to take reading seriously we discover that not all writers use the same words in the same way. To take a very obvious example, there are some writers who use a 'play on words' technique, deliberately employing a word with a double meaning to convey their intention. Often the intention is to be humorous. Such a writer, for instance, was Thomas Hood, who wrote many works in the 19th century, but who may best be remembered for his use of the *pun*. He wrote, for example, of the soldier, of whom, he said:

> But a cannon-ball took off his legs
> So he laid down his arms!

Such a use of a word's double meaning is only intelligible if our vocabulary extends to include such interpretations.

Communicating by implication
Often a writer intends us to understand his or her meaning to be quite different from the literal interpretation of the words used. Such a style of writing may be called 'communicating by *implication*' in which the writer may use a variety of hints, suggestions, innuendo, and ambiguity to convey a very different impression from that given by the surface appearance of the words.

Innuendo
This is described in the dictionary as an 'oblique remark', an 'allusive hint'—in other words, a phrase used to indicate something *other than* what the words would seem to say.

If, for instance, we hear or read of someone saying:

> 'He offered to pay what he owes by Christmas,
> and we all know what his promises mean, don't we!'

we have a distinct impression that the speaker does not think much of the debtor's promises! This may be unfair, as the speaker *may* mean that 'we all know that he is a man of his word' but the way the words have been used implies that the debtor is not to be trusted.

Ambiguity
This means 'a word or phrase capable of more than one meaning'. We had instances of this in the detective's 'solution' and in Thomas Hood's pun where the humour relies on his ambiguous use of the word 'arms'.

The writer's point of view
Another important factor to take into consideration when reading is the writer's point of view.

Writers may write in three ways: *objectively, subjectively*, or using a *blend of both styles*.

Objective writing.
When a writer writes objectively, we are likely to get an unprejudiced, impartial account or description of the subject.

For one thing, the writer leaves out any reference to him- or herself. The word 'I' rarely, if ever, occurs. Such a style is admirably suitable for reports and commentaries.

Subjective writing
The subjective writer's aim is to put ideas into our minds; to make us think and feel what he or she wants us to think or feel; to share with us emotions, views, attitudes and reactions so that we may come to think in the same way and to respond accordingly. Subjective writing is basically 'persuasive' writing.

It is important to be able to recognise the difference between an *objective* approach and a *subjective* one, and to realise, whilst we are reading or listening, how far the writer or speaker is seeking to influence our thinking or whether he or she is simply giving us information about which we must make up our own minds.

A blend
Perhaps our greatest problems occur when a writer blends both styles and writes partly objectively, partly subjectively. It is here that we have to think carefully, and exercise our judgement and powers of criticism.

Sometimes we are given a whole series of facts and figures in a purely objective manner and, before we realise it, the writer is trying to influence the way in which we interpret these facts.

When we come to look at the preparation of reports in Chapter 6, we shall be reminded of the very important distinction that is to be made between *fact* and *opinion*. At this stage, it is essential that we have a firm grasp of the distinction between objective and subjective writing, since this roughly approximates to the difference between fact and opinion.

Perhaps the best way of grasping this distinction is to examine writing of a subjective and persuasive nature such as *advertising,* and to notice how we are guided towards certain conclusions about particular products.

Advertising

First we must remind ourselves that the purpose of advertising is *not* to give us information but to encourage us to buy a product.

There are several methods of advertising open to businesses. It depends on whether or not the business concerned wishes to promote their product locally, nationally or even internationally.

If we look at *local advertising*, the most popular methods to use are the local press, local radio and television, and the house-to-house distribution of *circulars.*

Circulars are a kind of letter but usually take the form of a pamphlet or leaflet of some kind—colourful and designed to be eye-catching. They use a variety of *advertising gimmicks* to promote the product: colourful and attractive drawings, cartoons, pictures, etc.; a 'brash' and 'racy' style, including those magnetic words 'FREE OFFER!', 'NEW!', 'NO INTEREST CHARGED!'; freepost tear-off reply cards; famous personalities to promote the product; coupons that can be used in local stores and offers of free gifts. All of these gimmicks are designed to attract us to the product.

Let us look at the *use of words* in the following example:

'NINE OUT OF TEN WOMEN IN BRITAIN USE "SUDSY" ON WASHDAY!'

Surely if 'nine out of ten women in Britain' buy this product it must be something special! However, before we draw this conclusion, consider the wording again. We can read what the advertisement says, how about what it does *not* say?

The Trade Descriptions Act in Britain forbids advertisers to claim something for a product that is not true, so what the advertisers say is perfectly true—as far as it goes! What they do *not* say is that 'nine out of *every* ten women in Britain' use this product, because this would not be true! The omission of 'every' makes all the difference. After all, it would not be difficult to find ten women in Britain, nine of whom use the product.

Consider also the role of famous people in the promotion of products. Endorsement by a well-known person is meant to 'sell' you a product even though that person is usually not an expert on that particular product.

The same kind of false conclusion is sometimes encouraged by the information that the product has been greatly improved by the addition of a 'magic' ingredient.

There are so many ways in which advertisements set out to mislead us, that it would take a whole book to discuss them all.

The point is, that we need to *think* carefully about everything we hear and read. We need to look for what is not being said, and avoid being blinded by words, faulty arguments, or by a play on our emotions.

Questions

1 Describe three types of reading and write briefly on the purpose and usefulness of each.
2 Write a letter to a friend who does not know what a public library of today offers, telling him or her what services are available. (It would be more realistic if you first visited a large central library yourself and found out the facts at first hand.)
3 Using a dictionary or any other reference book, you should find out the meaning of the following Latin and French phrases still in common use. When you have the meanings, write out a short sentence in which the phrase is used correctly.

   ad infinitum; extempore; habeas corpus;
   modus operandi; nil desperandum; non sequitur;
   persona non grata; sine die; sub judice; vox populi.

   à la carte; bête noire; bon mot; fait accompli; idée fixe;
   poste restante; sangfroid; savoir-faire; table d'hôte;
   tête-à-tête.

4 Identify any *metaphors* or *similes* in the following account of an office fire:
   'A fire broke out in the office last week. It started in a wastepaper basket, but quickly took hold. Soon it was raging

fiercely, but fortunately the staff had time to leave the building safely. In spite of regular fire drills, some people panicked and started to run like rabbits, but they were soon calmed down by the example of others. The inferno was contained by the Fire Brigade, who arrived very speedily and who attacked the flames like a swarm of hornets defending a nest. An assessment of the damage was made quickly so that the bill could be prepared for the insurance company's consideration.'

5 Read the following extract from a report on the Annual General Meeting of a company during which the Chairman was to deliver his annual address. You may notice that it is written in the *objective* style, i.e. the writer of the report makes no reference to him or herself or to his or her personal feelings at the time.

Re-write this in the *subjective* style, as though you were the reporter, beginning with the phrase: 'When I attended the Annual General Meeting the Chairman was given, . . .' Keep more or less to the same wording, but write it from a personal point of view.

'The Chairman was given a standing ovation by the shareholders filling the large hall, as he rose to his feet to deliver the annual address.

His figure was tall and commanding, and he stood like a monolith, his hand raised in acknowledgement of the adulation until the reverberations of clapping and cheering had died away.

Only then did he begin to speak. The voice which came out of this great frame was ludicrously at odds with his leonine and majestic appearance. It was high-pitched—almost a squeak— and a little titter of laughter broke out, only to be quelled instantly by the stern and forbidding frowns of the old-stagers, who were intent only on hearing this harbinger of higher profits for the Company, and therefore greater dividends for the shareholders. They cared only for their emoluments, in whatever tone of voice they were announced!'

6 Write a brief explanation of the words underlined, as they are used in the context.

7 Write a letter to a friend who is about to start a course at college setting out what you think is important about *reading,* and what part you think it may play in preparing for a future career.

8 Give examples of at least two advertisements you think are misleading.

Chapter 4

A Look at Language

In the last chapter we looked at *reading*. Now we shall look at *writing* and, in particular, the various parts of speech that are the building blocks of our language. However, it is worth looking first at the ways in which written English differs from spoken English. English speakers tend to tolerate errors in speech, but to expect 'correct' and competent writing skills.

Spoken English (for people for whom it is their native language) is learned by children from the adults around them, and later from school friends who speak according to the local patterns (e.g. accent, idioms, colloquialisms, etc.), which may stray from standard written English.

Some examples will show the unacceptable uses of spoken English when put into writing:

(a) In some parts of Britain you can hear the question 'Where *be* you going?' Clearly this is not an acceptable use of the verb 'to be'. It should be *written* as 'Where *are* you going?'

(b) In some conversations you can hear the sentence 'I *aren't* going to do that'. Again, this is an unacceptable use of the verb 'to be'. It should be *written* as 'I *am* not going to do that'.

This does not mean that one has to learn a lot of rules about grammar and syntax (sentence construction) before one can write acceptably. However, there are certain basic *conventions* or *standards* of written English that one cannot afford to ignore if one's written communication is to be widely understood.

If you are to work as a secretary or clerical worker it *is* important that you are really competent in the use of English. You may need to correct a letter or some other document in which mistakes have been made, or you may have to compose a report or memo yourself. Remember that bad writing gives a very poor impression, both of the writer and of the firm he or she works for.

Just as we cannot expect to make or repair a car or motor-cycle until we have learned the difference between the parts of the engine, so we cannot hope to build proper sentences until we know the materials we have to work with, and how to put them together.

4.1   Sentences

A sentence is the expression of *one idea*. Any sentence that contains more than one idea is incorrect. For example, 'My sister is older than I.' and 'When we went on holiday last year it rained all the time.' are complete sentences. To put both these unconnected statements into one sentence, 'My sister is older than I and it rained all the time we were on holiday last year.' is incorrect.

What does a sentence consist of?

The very least that a sentence *must* have is a *subject* and a *verb*. Without both of these, the words used do not make a proper sentence. The third element often required in sentence construction is an *object*.

What is the subject?

Subject has several meanings. In sentence construction it means 'the person or thing *doing the action*'.

What is the verb?

It is the *action being done*. This may be in the past, present or future.

What is the object?

The *object* of the verb is the person or thing acted upon by the verb. For instance, in the sentence *The child throws the stick*:

'The child' is the *subject* (the person doing the action)
'throws'   is the *verb*   (the action being done)
'the stick' is the *object* (the thing acted upon).

We can add to this sentence. For example, perhaps *The child throws the stick for the dog*. We have now introduced something that is involved in the action, but that is not directly acted upon by the verb. In the above sentence the dog is the *indirect object*.

Before we proceed any further, let us look at how the points made above work out in practice. For instance, most of us will know the following nursery rhyme:

> Hey diddle diddle, the cat and the fiddle.
> The cow jumped over the moon.
> The little dog laughed to see such fun,
> and the dish ran away with the spoon!

Analysing the first line of this rhyme:

> Hey diddle diddle, the cat and the fiddle.

shows that it is *not a sentence at all*. It contains *no action word* (or *verb*). It is simply a *phrase* and should not be used by itself as though it were a sentence. The second line:

> The cow jumped over the moon.

is a perfectly good sentence. It has a subject 'The cow', a verb 'jumped' and an object 'the moon'.

The third and fourth lines would be good sentences if they were separated by a full-stop, but unfortunately, being joined by the word 'and', they express two totally unconnected ideas combined into one statement, and this is bad English.

There are two exceptions to the rule that a phrase should not stand by itself. One of these is when we are writing down a conversation. When speaking with people, especially when answering questions, the answers are often in phrases, and not in sentences. For example, if someone asked 'Who were present at Cinderella's Ball?' the answer could be 'The cat and the fiddle!' This is not a sentence, though it would be a permissible verbal answer. So we can use 'phrases' when reporting conversation.

The second use of phrases by themselves is in *titles*. 'The Cat and the Fiddle' could be a title but we still need to recognise that it is *not* a sentence!

The following diagram shows how the 'building blocks' of language fit together.

The bricks for sentence building

VERBS	NOUNS	PRONOUNS	
	ADVERBS	ADJECTIVES	ARTICLES
PREPOSITIONS	CONJUNCTIONS	INTERJECTIONS	

Now let us look more closely at the *parts of speech* or 'building materials' from which sentences are constructed.

4.2   Nouns

These are *naming words*. They *name* anything; days of the week, festivals, actions, attitudes, things, and, of course, people.

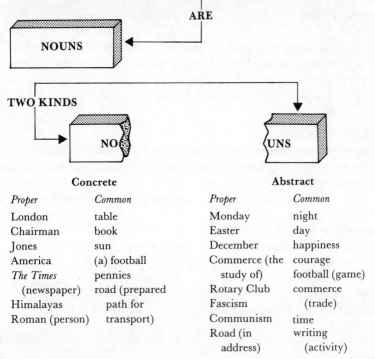

WORDS THAT **NAME** THINGS, PEOPLE, PLACES, ACTIVITIES, DAYS, MONTHS, SPECIAL EVENTS, SUBJECTS, TITLES

ARE

NOUNS

TWO KINDS

NOUNS

Concrete		Abstract	
Proper	*Common*	*Proper*	*Common*
London	table	Monday	night
Chairman	book	Easter	day
Jones	sun	December	happiness
America	(a) football	Commerce (the	courage
The Times	pennies	study of)	football (game)
(newspaper)	road (prepared	Rotary Club	commerce
Himalayas	path for	Fascism	(trade)
Roman (person)	transport)	Communism	time
		Road (in	writing
		address)	(activity)

There are four types of noun—(a) concrete, (b) proper, (c) abstract and (d) collective.

If these names are confusing, do not worry about them. The names are not very important; what we should recognise is what the differences are.

Concrete nouns

These are simply the names of things that we can see, and touch and recognise by our physical senses—like table, chair or pen.

Proper nouns
These are special names, such as Wednesday, Christmas, Birmingham, Alf Jones or Buckingham Palace. These names should always begin with a capital letter.

Abstract nouns
These are the nouns that cause the most problems, since they are the names of attitudes or qualities, such as courage, hatred, anxiety, action, bewilderment, etc. Sometimes they are mistaken for verbs because they seem to be 'action words'. For example, although 'singing' is often used as a verb, as in the phrase 'she was singing loudly', it becomes a noun when we write the phrase 'singing was her main hobby', because then we have changed the use of the word 'singing' from an action to an *activity*.

Collective nouns
These are nouns that name a group of people or animals or things. For example, we speak of a 'committee', or a 'team', or a 'Government'.

You may find difficulty in deciding whether to treat the group as a *single* thing or as a *number* of individuals. In some instances it does not really matter. In the sentence 'The Government decided that *it should* (or *they should*) take action.' you can treat the Government as a single unit or as a group of individuals. But there are instances when common sense tells you that to treat the group as *singular* would be wrong. For example, it would be nonsense to write: 'When the team played abroad *it* took *its* wives with *it*.'

4.3   Pronouns

Pronouns stand in place of nouns. In English nouns do not change, wherever they stand in a sentence, unless they are in the possessive case, when they require an apostrophe. Pronouns, however, do change their form. Take, for example, the sentence: 'The girl typed a letter to her boyfriend'. We can replace the nouns 'girl' and 'boyfriend' with pronouns, so that it reads: *She* typed a letter to *him*. But we could use other pronouns. Why, for instance, do we not say: *Her* typed a letter to *he*?

You may answer that 'this doesn't sound right' but this is not the real reason. The real reason lies in what was said earlier about the *subject* and *object* in sentence construction. Pronouns can be divided into three groups, which look like this:

SUBJECT CASE	OBJECT CASE	POSSESSIVE CASE
I	me	mine
you	you	yours
he, she, it, one	him, her, it, one	his, hers, its, one's
we	us	ours
you	you	yours
they	them	theirs

As you will see, this table tells us which pronoun to use when we want to replace a noun, remembering the rule that *a noun working as the subject of a sentence must be replaced by a subject case pronoun*. Equally, we replace a noun that names the object of a verb by an *object case* pronoun.

Let us see how using this table works out in practice.

Suppose that someone knocks at the door. You will probably call out, 'Who's there?'. The chances are that a familiar voice will reply, 'It's me'.

We accept this without questioning the 'correctness' of the English, because it has become quite acceptable *in speech* to use this kind of wording. In *writing*, however, it would not be acceptable, because it is quite wrong!

The phrase involves a personal pronoun (me) and it also involves a verb (It is which is contracted to It's)—which is part of the verb 'to be'.

There is a rule in English that states: *Any personal pronoun following any part of the verb 'to be' must be in the subject case.*

The reply given above used an *object case* pronoun (me) when it should have been the *subject case* (I). The reply should therefore have been 'It's I', but this sounds uncomfortable so we *say* 'It's me'.

If we think what the whole sentence is that your friend is saying, 'It's me' means 'Me am knocking at the door', and this is clearly not correct. Extension into a whole sentence in this way will help you to follow the rule correctly. In *speech* use of the wrong case may be permissible, but never in *writing*. For example, in a letter we may see something like:

> Smith & Jones were also involved in this deal. If anything has gone wrong, I'm sure it was not us to blame, it was *them*.

Look at the table above, and you will see that 'them' is an *object case* pronoun. What should the writer have written?

There is another important rule concerning personal pronouns. It concerns the verb 'to let' (permit, allow). *After the verb 'to let' any personal pronoun must be in the object case.*

The most frequent error made in this respect is with the phrase 'you and I'. If the word 'let' or 'permit' or 'allow' stands in front of this phrase, it should be '*you* and *me*', and *both* these pronouns are from the *object case* column in the table.

'Let you and I go to the party' sounds all right, but is wrong. It should be 'Let *you* and *me* go to the party'.

'They won't allow you or I to vote until we are 18' sounds all right, but should be '. . . *you* or *me* . . .'.

This same rule also applies whenever we use the word *between*. We often hear someone say, 'Just between you and I . . .' Wrong! 'Just between you and me . . .' is the correct form.

Possessive pronouns (and possessive adjectives)

If you examine the column headed *Possessive Case*, in the table shown, you will notice that apart from 'mine', all the possessive case personal pronouns end in 's'. This may lead you to ask: 'What about words like my, your, our and their? Are not these also possessive pronouns?' The answer is that strictly speaking, they are *not*; they are possessive *adjectives*.

Pronouns *replace* nouns; the words in your question do not replace nouns, they are used *with* a noun, therefore they cannot be *pro-nouns* (i.e. *for* a noun).

If we write: 'This is *your* book', the word 'your' is an adjective. If we write 'This is *yours*' we are using yours as a pronoun, and the noun has disappeared.

Notice, also, that with the exception of 'one's', *no possessive pronoun has an apostrophe*. If we write 'The dog had injured *it's* paw', the word '*it's*' (with an apostrophe), meaning 'it *is* or, it *has*', makes nonsense of the statement.

You may be wondering what the point is of learning all about possessive pronouns and possessive adjectives. Perhaps the next point will make clear how important it is to be aware of the different functions words serve when we are writing.

One of the commonest causes of error is the confusion between *there, their* and *they're,* which all sound the same. The error is avoided if you know the difference between the meanings of these words. You should know the following:

There is an *adverb* and usually indicates a place, as in: 'She lived *there* for many years'. It can also be used at the beginning of a sentence to draw attention to, or point out, someone or something: 'There's the book I lost!'.

Their is a *possessive adjective,* and means 'of them' or 'belonging to them', as in 'She was *their* long-lost sister whom they had not seen since they were children'.

They're is a *contraction* of the two words *they* and *are*—the subject case of a pronoun plus part of the verb 'to be'. For example: 'Bill and Jenny are twins. *They're* moving from the district soon.' We should *not* use contractions as a general rule in business letters or documents, although they are used freely in speech.

4.4 Adjectives

An adjective is used to modify a noun. It is a describing word, used *only* with nouns—not with any other word. Most words, therefore, that stand in front of a noun or qualify or add to it in some way are adjectives. These include the possessive adjectives, such as 'my, your, his, her, our, their', and also the words sometimes called 'articles': 'the' and 'a' (or 'an'). These too, are working as adjectives when they stand in front of a noun. Neither the possessive adjectives nor the articles look like 'proper' adjectives, but we must always look at a word's function and identify it by the role it plays within a sentence. For example, the word 'talking' may look like a verb, but in the phrase 'the *talking* doll' it is working as an *adjective!*

There are three forms that an adjective can take: simple, comparative and superlative.

SIMPLE	COMPARATIVE	SUPERLATIVE
fat	fat-ter	fat-test
small	small-er	small-est
tiny	tini-er	tini-est

Apart from the small spelling changes to the words, the general pattern is to add '-er' to form the comparative (when we are speaking of only *two*) and '-est' to form the superlative (when speaking of *more than two*). The comparative is used only for *two* things or people, e.g. 'Susan is the taller of the two sisters.' The superlative is used for *more than two* things or people, e.g. 'She is the tallest girl in the group.' However, some adjectives cannot be used in this way. For example, 'incredible' and 'beautiful' cannot be written or spoken of as 'incredibler' or 'beautifullest'!

In these instances we have to use *more* and *most* to form the comparative and superlative. However, it is wrong to use these words with anything other than the *simple* form of the adjective. It is wrong, for example, to speak of the 'more fatter of the two' or the 'most fattest boy in the class'. If you listen to people talking you will often hear this error being made. 'It is the most easiest thing in the world' someone may say. This is quite incorrect.

There is no difference between 'elder' and 'older'; 'eldest' and 'oldest', but the usual practice is to use 'elder' and 'eldest' only for members of the same family or tribe. 'Elder' has more than one meaning, so look it up and note the differences.

Certain adjectives have more than one meaning in their comparative and superlative forms, for example

LATE	LATER	LATEST
	LATTER	LAST

We have to be rather careful when using these adjectives as what we say (or write) and what we mean to say (or write) may be different. For example, it may be very pleasing for an author to be told that 'your *latest* book was very enjoyable', but to say 'your *last* book was very enjoyable' sounds ominous—as if the author were not expected to write another!

Finally, one of the commonest mistakes occurs when we use an adjective as an adverb, for example, 'You are walking too quick for me'. 'Quick' is an adjective, but it is being misused here to modify the verb 'are walking'. The word we need is 'quick*ly*', which is an adverb.

4.5   Verbs

One of the facts about English that most people remember from school-days is that the verb is the *action* or *'doing' word* in a sentence.

What seems to be less well remembered, is that there are *two* different kinds of verb—one that can stand by itself, requiring no object to complete it. These verbs are called 'intransitive' and are indicated in the dictionary by the letters (v.i.) after the verb. The other kind *does* require an object. These are called 'transitive' and are indicated by the letters (v.t.) in the dictionary. Some verbs can fall into both categories.

Examples of *intransitive* verbs are: laugh, sleep, dream, as in 'I laughed. He slept. She dreamed.'

Examples of *transitive* verbs are: kick, give, say, as in 'He kicked . . . (what?); I gave . . . (what?); She said . . . (what?).'

Parts of the verb
Verbs have many parts, some of which we call 'tenses', others have special names of their own. The table on page 50 shows the principal parts of the verbs 'walk' and 'write'.

The following set of notes is intended to condense and simplify information on the different parts of verbs. The intention here is to point out the errors that occur most frequently, and how to avoid them.

The infinitive
This consists of the word 'to', followed by the basic verb, which is the present tense, hence *'to + write'*.

The error easily committed here is to 'split' the infinitive by inserting another word *between* the *to* and the *verb,* e.g. 'to *quickly* write'. Splitting the infinitive is best avoided. The inserted word should be placed *before* or *after* the infinitive, e.g. 'quickly to write' or 'to write quickly'.

The present tense
This expresses an action going on at the present time, e.g. 'I write . . .'. The 'persons' of the verb are all the subject case personal pronouns. The only change in the present tense occurs in the third person singular (he, she, it, one) after which the verb usually takes an 's', e.g. he write*s*.

The past tense
This also uses the subject case personal pronouns, but this tense requires *no* change in the third person singular. However, the verb itself changes form, e.g. He *wrote.* This should not be confused with the *past participle* form.

Parts of the verb

INFINITIVE: TO WALK **PRESENT PARTICIPLE: WALKING** **PAST PARTICIPLE: WALKED**

	PRESENT SIMPLE	PRESENT CONTINUOUS	FUTURE SIMPLE	PAST SIMPLE	PAST CONTINUOUS	PERFECT SIMPLE
I	walk	am walking	shall walk	walked	was walking	have walked
YOU	walk	are walking	will walk	walked	were walking	have walked
HE/SHE	walks	is walking	will walk	walked	was walking	has walked
WE	walk	are walking	shall walk	walked	were walking	have walked
YOU	walk	are walking	will walk	walked	were walking	have walked
THEY	walk	are walking	will walk	walked	were walking	have walked

INFINITIVE: TO WRITE **PRESENT PARTICIPLE: WRITING** **PAST PARTICIPLE: WRITTEN**

	PRESENT SIMPLE	PRESENT CONTINUOUS	FUTURE SIMPLE	PAST SIMPLE	PAST CONTINUOUS	PERFECT SIMPLE
I	write	am writing	shall write	wrote	was writing	have written
YOU	write	are writing	will write	wrote	were writing	have written
HE/SHE	writes	is writing	will write	wrote	was writing	has written
WE	write	are writing	shall write	wrote	were writing	have written
YOU	write	are writing	will write	wrote	were writing	have written
THEY	write	are writing	will write	wrote	were writing	have written

The future tense
There are *two* future tenses in English. One is called 'simple' and the other 'determined'. The first implies 'all being well'; the second is used when we imply 'come what may' and is more in the nature of an order or command. You can see from the table that the 'simple' form uses 'shall, will, will; shall, will, will) while the 'determined' form is the other way round, (will, shall, shall; will, shall, shall).

The form of the verb does *not* change in the third person singular.

The present participle
This is the part of a verb that is the easiest to recognise in a sentence since all present participles end in—ing. For example, he was walk-ing (past continuous); I am walk-ing (present continuous). Although these examples refer to past and present actions, they both use *present* participles. In these examples the present participle is working as a *verb*; but note carefully the following points that we should remember when handling the present participle:

(a) In a phrase such as: 'The walking man . . .' it is working as an *adjective* (describing the noun 'man'), and in a sentence such as 'I like walking' it is working as a *noun*, i.e. it is naming an activity not actually taking place.

(b) If the present participle *begins* a sentence or a phrase, the person or thing doing that action (i.e. the *subject*) must be placed *as soon as possible after it*, otherwise it causes ambiguity. For example, *'Having* written the letter, the post office was found to be closed' should be *'Having* written the letter, *I* found the post office closed. This error is known as the 'misrelated participle', as the person really doing the action is either not named at all, or named after the reader has been confused by another noun or pronoun nearer the participle.

(c) The third point about present participles is rather more difficult to understand. When a present participle functions as a noun (as in she likes *walking*) it is called a *gerund* or verbal-noun.

Let us imagine that your employer says: 'I don't like you taking so much time off!'

In this example, is the present participle 'taking' working as a verb, an adjective or a noun (or noun-phrase)? How can one be sure?

The answer depends on three little words—'the idea of'! If you can fit these words into the sentence and still make sense then you can be sure that the present participle is working as a noun (or its equivalent).

If we look again at what your employer says, and try the phrase 'the idea of', we find it reads: 'I don't like *the idea of* you taking so much time off'.

Once we are sure that this present participle is a *gerund,* we can apply the following rule: *any noun or pronoun preceding a gerund must be in the possessive case.* In the above example the pronoun is in the *object* case and is therefore incorrect. Your employer should have said: 'I dislike *your* taking so much time off!' After all, it is not *you* he dislikes, it is *your taking so much time off* (a noun-phrase).

To see this more clearly, we have only to substitute a more recognisable noun for the noun-phrase. He might have said: 'I do not like *your* dress'. 'Dress' is clearly a *noun,* and he would not dream of saying: 'I do not like *you* dress'.

The same rule applies when we use people's names. 'I don't like Janet being given that promotion' we may say, begrudgingly. What we should have said was: 'I don't like *Janet's* being given that promotion.' Can you see why we have to use the possessive case? Try and work it out; it is a bit complicated at first, but if you follow the reasoning step by step you will see the logic of the rule.

The past participle

This is not as complicated as the present participle, but it does create several problems.

(a) The past participle is used to form several tenses such as the present perfect simple. However, it is a very *different* word from that used in the past simple, though many people fall into the trap of using the past simple form. So you hear them say, 'I have *wrote* . . .'; 'I have *rang* . . .', etc. A great many verbs in English have a very different form for the past participle e.g. 'wrote' in the past simple becomes 'have *written*' in the present perfect simple; 'rang' in the past simple becomes 'have *rung*' in the present perfect simple. If a past participle has the same form as the past simple, as in *'walked'* and 'have *walked'* we should regard this as purely coincidental and certainly *not* as a rule!

(b) Some people are confused in the opposite way—they mix up the past participle with the past tense, so we hear (or read) 'I *seen . . .*'; 'They've *went . . .*', etc.

(c) You will have noticed that the present perfect simple tense is formed by using the verb 'to have' (I have; you have; he/she/it/one has, etc.). In speech we often shorten or contract this to 've' as in I've, you've, we've, they've, etc.

This often gives rise to a serious error, perhaps through the influence of our speech, when we write (and say) *of* instead of *have*. This is most likely to occur when we use words such as 'may, might, could, would, should, etc.', which then appear as, 'might *of* . . .; could *of* . . .; should *of* . . ., etc.' We should not combine *of* with the words listed above. The word to use is *have*.

4.6 Adverbs

Adverbs can qualify, modify or alter in some way every part of speech except nouns and pronouns; adverbs can even modify other adverbs (see page 54).

4.7 Prepositions

Prepositions are those words that link two or more nouns by stating the relationship between them. If this sounds rather complicated it may be made clearer if you think of the word *preposition* as telling us of the position between two or more things or people, e.g. 'He walked *by* the desk' (see page 55).

Perhaps the commonest error occurs when the preposition is allowed to separate from its noun or pronoun—and this is most clearly seen with the pronoun 'who'.

Few people fail to write 'by whom; with whom; for whom' because the preposition stands in front of the pronoun. However, many fail to make the same adjustment when other words separate the pronoun from the preposition. Consequently, they say or write:

'*Who* shall I give this *to*?'
'*Who* did you go *with*?'

when they should use the object case pronoun *whom*.

The result of combining the preposition with the pronoun is to sound stilted, unnatural and pompous:

'*To whom* shall I give this?'
'*With whom* did you go?'

So if you prefer to use natural forms, putting the preposition at the end, remember to use *whom* and not *who*.

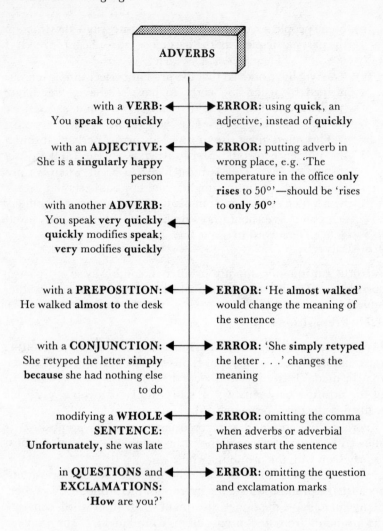

with a **VERB:** ◄—————► **ERROR:** using **quick**, an
You **speak** too **quickly**   adjective, instead of **quickly**

with an **ADJECTIVE:** ◄—————► **ERROR:** putting adverb in
She is a **singularly happy**   wrong place, e.g. 'The
person   temperature in the office **only
rises** to 50°'—should be 'rises
with another **ADVERB:**   to **only 50°**'
You speak **very quickly**
quickly modifies **speak**;
very modifies **quickly**

with a **PREPOSITION:** ◄—————► **ERROR:** 'He **almost walked**'
He walked **almost to** the desk   would change the meaning of
the sentence

with a **CONJUNCTION:** ◄—————► **ERROR:** 'She **simply retyped**
She retyped the letter **simply**   the letter . . .' changes the
because she had nothing else   meaning
to do

modifying a **WHOLE** ◄—————► **ERROR:** omitting the comma
SENTENCE: when adverbs or adverbial
Unfortunately, she was late   phrases start the sentence

in **QUESTIONS** and ◄—————► **ERROR:** omitting the question
EXCLAMATIONS: and exclamation marks
'**How** are you?'

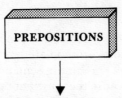

PREPOSITIONS

Preposition means **standing in front of** and normally a preposition stands in front of a noun (or pronoun).

Common prepositions are:

above	during	to
after	for	towards
against	from	upon
along	in	under(neath)
around	off	with
at	on	without
before (in front of)	over	
behind	since	
below (under)	through	
beside		
between		

4.8 Conjunctions

Conjunctions join sentences together when the sentences are about the same thing. The most common are 'and' and 'but'. However, there are lots of ways of combining sentences (called 'synthesis'); these are important because they prevent our style or writing from becoming 'jerky'.

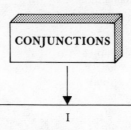

CONJUNCTIONS

I

Sentences must not be joined together unless they are about the same topic. There has to be unity between the two or more statements.

e.g. The Secretary will be taking her holidays in July, and it was raining in Manchester last Friday.

Clearly, the two completely unrelated ideas in the above should not be joined in one sentence.

II

A comma is not a conjunction; we must not use it to join statements. For example, it would be incorrect to write:

I have made a mistake, I could not help it, I was distracted by the telephone ringing.

Instead we can use *(a)* conjunctions:
I have made a mistake *but* I could not help it *because* I was distracted . . .
or *(b)* semi-colons:
I have made a mistake; I could not help it; I was distracted . . .
or *(c)* three separate sentences:
I have made a mistake. I could not help it. I was distracted . . .

There are three kinds of conjunction:

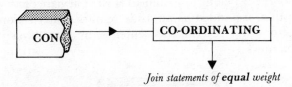

*Join statements of **equal** weight*

Jane went to College. Julie went to College.
Jane **and** Julie went to College.
Some other co-ordinating conjunctions are: **but, however, nevertheless, or, otherwise, then, therefore, yet.**

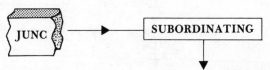

*Used when one part of a sentence **depends** on another*

They passed their exams. They worked hard.
They passed their exams **because** they worked hard.
Some other subordinating conjunctions are: **after, although, before, if, since, that, unless, until, where, while.**

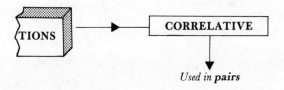

*Used in **pairs***

She was good at typing. She was good at shorthand.
Not only was she good at typing **but** she was **also** good at shorthand.
(**Also** must be included, but may be placed in any appropriate position.)
Some other correlative conjunctions are: **either . . . or, neither . . . nor, if . . . then, both . . . and, not merely . . . but even, whether . . . or.**

4.9   Interjections

These do not really belong to sentences at all. They are those words or phrases that are added as an aside remark. Interjections are separated from the rest of the sentence by a comma or an exclamation mark.

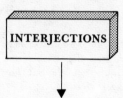

are not really part of a sentence, and may be omitted without any loss of meaning

should always be separated by an exclamation mark or a comma from the rest of the sentence

should not be included in reported speech or in summaries

Examples

'**Ouch!** I've just knocked my knee!'

'**Alas,** I wish I'd known beforehand.'

'Pass the salt, **please, Mother**.'

'**Sir,** your caller has arrived.'

'**Ladies and gentlemen,** it gives me great pleasure to . . .'

'I think this is yours, **Janet**.'

'**Hooray!** I've been given an extra holiday!'

It is worth learning these eight parts of speech. Remember, however, that this is only the *classification* of words. They can move from class to class depending on how they are used in sentences.

These are the 'building bricks' for sentence construction. Just as we would find it almost impossible to build a car engine without learning the difference between a carburettor and an exhaust pipe, so we cannot master the mechanics of the English language if we have not understood the difference between the materials (words) available to us.

It is absolutely essential to be competent in English for anyone wanting to make a career in business, industry or commerce. Of course, there are always exceptional people who somehow 'get to the top' without language skill, but they are the exceptions that prove the rule. Most of us have to do it the hard way and this requires courage and self-discipline. The real question we have to answer is not 'Is the work hard?', but 'Is it satisfying and worthwhile?'

Questions

1 Correct any of the following that you think are wrong:
   (a) 'It wasn't you, it wasn't me, it wasn't her. So who's to blame?'
   (b) 'Do you think the manager will let you and I off on Wednesday to go to the International match?'
   (c) He drove fast up the motorway because he had a fast car. (Explain what you think the difference is between the words 'fast'.)
   (d) Sheila can write quicker shorthand than her. In fact Sheila was the most fastest at shorthand in the college.
   (e) 'Here, let you and me have a go!'
   (f) Her father doesn't like the idea of him keeping her out at night after 11 p.m.
2 Explain the difference between a 'transitive' and an 'intransitive' verb. Give examples other than those in the chapter.
3 'She is not only a good typist, but she is good at shorthand.' What is missing from this sentence?

Chapter 5

Punctuation

Punctuation is to the written word what facial expression, gesture and tone of voice are to the spoken word. It supplies additional information. Moreover it breaks up the flow of words into comprehensible units—sentences, phrases and clauses.

5.1 The Full Stop

A full stop marks the end of a sentence. After a full stop we should begin the next statement with a capital letter. This is learned at school from an early age. What we often do *not* learn are the other uses of the full stop.

One of the other major uses of the full stop is to indicate *abbreviations*. It was once customary to use a full stop after such abbreviations as Mr. (Mister); Rd. (Road); Ave. (Avenue); Dr. (Doctor or Debtor), etc. Such words are no longer regarded as abbreviations, and now we see Mr, Rd, Ave and Dr without the full stop. We now distinguish between an abbreviation and a *contraction*. The rule is quite simple: If a 'short form' of a word contains the *first* and *last* letters of the shortened word, it is a *contraction* and needs *no* full stop. If the word does *not* show the first and last letters it is treated as an *abbreviation* and needs a full stop, for example: etc. (etcetera), Cresc. (Crescent) or Yorks. (Yorkshire).

It is now common to omit the full stop between letters showing degrees, awards or qualifications, for example FRSA (instead of F.R.S.A.) and MIME (instead of M.I.M.E.).

The omission of the full stop from certain names of organisations or scientific processes has created a new kind of word. For instance, the North Atlantic Treaty Organization, which used to be written as N.A.T.O., is now written NATO and is pronounced as one word. Similarly, Radio Detection and Ranging was abbreviated to

R.A.D.A.R. and then contracted to RADAR and pronounced as one word. Such words are known as *acronyms.*

5.2 The Comma

The comma is one of the most troublesome punctuation marks and as a result it is either used too much or not enough.

Perhaps the most common error is to use the comma as a conjunction, i.e. to *join* sentences or statements together. The comma does *not* join sentences, it *separates* them. To write, 'I went to Spain last year, the weather was very hot, the temperature reached 100 degrees most days.' is incorrect. Since commas do not join we have three options when writing these statements:

(a) We can write them as *separate sentences,* using full-stops.

(b) We can use conjunctions such as 'and' and 'but', etc.

(c) We can use a semi-colon (;) instead of conjunctions, for example, 'I went to Spain last year; the weather was very hot; the temperature reached 100 degrees most days.' (See Section 5.3.)

Another common error is to use a comma unnecessarily, as in, 'He said that, he thought it was going to rain.'

Correct uses of the comma

(1) To separate items in a *list,* for example, 'In my work-box I have needles, tape, press-studs and pins'. A comma may be inserted or omitted before the 'and' unless the final two items go together by association (e.g. knife and fork, fish and chips), when it should always be omitted.

(2) To separate *adjectives* when there are more than two, for example, 'He was a tall, dark, handsome man', *but no comma* in 'He was a dark and handsome man'.)

(3) To separate a *subordinate clause* from the rest of the sentence. A subordinate clause is a group of words that could be omitted from a sentence without the sentence losing meaning.For example, 'The clerk, who stammered very badly, dealt with our papers'. In this example, all we wish to say is that 'The clerk dealt with our papers'. If we wish to draw attention to the *particular* clerk whom we identify by his stammer, we omit the commas, thus, 'The clerk who stammered very badly dealt with our papers'.

(4) Commas should always be used after adverbs when they occur at the beginning of a sentence. For example, 'Unfortunately, the athlete was taken ill'.

(5) It is often better to use commas rather than *brackets,* as too many sets of brackets on a page can be distracting to the reader, who tends to look at the brackets first and not see the text as a whole. For example, 'Mr Brown (our lecturer in Law) was married last week', may equally be written: 'Mr Brown, our lecturer in Law, was married last week.'

5.3   The Semi-Colon

Many people do not know how to use this punctuation mark. It can be used in a number of ways.

It separates groups of items in a list. For example, suppose you were going shopping and wanted a number of items for the garden, the kitchen and the bathroom. A written account of this expedition might include something like this: 'For the garden, I bought six packets of seeds and a new trowel, a spade, and a sprinkler for the lawn; for the kitchen, I bought a cheese-grater, a milk-pan, and a roll of baking foil; for the bathroom, three tablets of soap, a face-cloth, and a bottle of disinfectant.' Notice how the groups are separated and how the use of commas only would have been inadequate because commas already are used as separation *within* the groups.

A semi-colon can also join sentences in the place of a conjunction. 'I have a typewriter. It does not spell very well!' could be written as, 'I have a typewriter; it does not spell very well!' instead of using 'and' or 'but'. (What we must *not* use, of course, is a comma!)

You must make sure, however, that any two (or more) statements you join together, either by conjunctions or semi-colons, are connected. For example, the two statements: 'My typewriter was a present from my aunt' and 'My new dress is a beautiful shade of blue' are not related so should not be joined together.

5.4   The Colon

Just as the semi-colon separates groups of items, so the colon separates 'groups of groups', i.e. when a list is not only divided into groups, but when there is a division needed between one group and the next.

The following is an extract from an estate agent's description of a house for sale. Notice the way in which the various groups are separated by the colon:

```
The property is a semi-detached bungalow consisting of a kitchen,
two bedrooms, a sitting-room, bathroom and toilet, and there are small
gardens at the front and rear of the premises.  The kitchen contains a
cooker (electric), refrigerator, and numerous power points; it is
decorated appropriately; the floor is wood; the ceiling is not papered,
but treated with a fire-resistant chemical: the two bedrooms are both
large enough to contain double or twin beds, and a wardrobe and dressing
table; the rooms have been decorated recently; the ceilings are tiled
with polystyrene tiles; the bedroom floor-coverings will be left by the
present owner: the sitting room may need redecorating, but is large and
spacious and faces south-east, so catches a lot of sun: the bathroom
is in excellent condition: the gardens are mature and have been well
cared for.  The whole premises are heated by ..... etc.
```

Colons can also be used to introduce lists, examples, quotations, etc. For example: 'The team selected for next Saturday's match will be: . . .'; 'The examples given in the text were: . . .'; 'Julius Caesar's well-known reply was: . . .'. The colon should always be used after phrases such as 'the following:'.

In 'balanced' phrases or sentences, where two or more parts of equal value are joined together one should use a colon. For example, 'Three times he tried: three times he failed'.

5.5 Brackets

Brackets are used when a quantity or a sum of money is expressed in words after the figures. For example, £300 (three hundred pounds).

They are also used to indicate that words are 'in parentheses', which means they are an aside. For example, 'This deal (providing it is completed in time) should be to the benefit of us all'. Not only can brackets often be replaced by commas (see above) but also by *dashes*.

5.6 The Apostrophe

This causes many problems; many people are unsure whether to put the apostrophe before or after the final 's' of a possessive word. To guarantee that we do this correctly we must ask 'Just what *is* an apostrophe, and why is it used?'

The answer to this is very important: an apostrophe always indicates that one or more letters are *missing* from a word!

The next point to grasp is that there are *two* kinds of word from which a letter has been removed.

(a) *Contractions.* These are words like 'I've, won't, can't, they're, who's (meaning 'who is' or 'who has') and so on. It is obvious which letter or letters have been omitted, and the apostrophe is put in the place of those letters.

(b) *Possessive Nouns,* such as Michael's hat, the two girls' dresses, London's traffic, children's books, a week's holiday, two weeks' holiday, etc. The placing of the apostrophe is not so obvious and, in any case, you may be wondering what letter or letters can be missing from these possessive nouns. The answer is to be found in the language of Chaucer or Spenser. Geoffrey Chaucer was born in 1340 and died in 1400. His best-known work is *The Canterbury Tales.* Edmund Spenser lived in the 16th century and is credited with being one of the greatest contributors to the English language. His best-known work is *The Faerie Queen.* The reason why we are interested in these two is that in those early days, when a noun was 'possessive' no apostrophe was used. The possessive noun simply *added* the letters –*es* to the end of the word, so they wrote 'Michaeles hat, the two girlses dresses, Londones traffic, and so on.

Eventually the 'e' and sometimes the 'es' were dropped, and so the apostrophe was used to show that a *letter or letters were missing!*

Consequently, to know where to put the apostrophe in phrases such as 'in a weeks time' and 'in two weeks time', you simply need to find out whether the time period is a single week (of a week, one week's time) or more than one week (of two weeks, two weeks' time).

Do not be confused by 'singulars' and 'plurals'. Plurals do not always end in 's' in English. For example, 'childrens games'— children is a plural that does not end in 's', so the correct punctuation is 'children's games'.

Note that if there is more than one name in a firm's or company's name the apostrophe is used only in the *last* name, e.g. Smith, Brown & Robinson's; Woolworth's (the shop of Woolworth); Marks and Spencer's, etc.

The only way to absorb and understand the rules of language and punctuation is to study each section carefully until you are sure you know the functions of each part of speech and punctuation mark.

Keep trying the following questions, and if you make errors, go back and study the relevant portions of the chapter until you have the correct answers.

Questions

1 What is the main purpose of punctuation?
2 What is the difference between an abbreviation and a contraction?
3 Correct, and put the apostrophes in, the following sentences:
   - (a) 'My boss sometimes makes me type Janes letters over again in the Managers office. Im sure yours wouldnt make you do that, would he?'
   - (b) Theyll be able to answer the phone when its repaired. Their going to repair it today, all being well.'
   - (c) Whos got my correcting fluid? Ive forgotten who I lent it to.'
   - (d) 'I went to Majorca last year, Im hoping to go again this year, I like the hot weather, the food isnt too bad.'
4 Punctuate and correct the following:

im not sure said the manager to his assistant that we should send that new girl to collage as she seems to be quite competant i think she needs to go replied the assistant as she makes a lot of mistakes when shes writing or typing english shes supposed to have an o level said the manager but i expect shes had no real training in business english whats the best day of the week for her to go do you think wednesday replied the assistant because were very busy every other day and i dont like mary being away when theirs a lot to do

Chapter 6

English at Work

In the last two chapters we looked at the rules of grammar and punctuation. These are your basic equipment as a writer, so study the different sections of Chapters 4 and 5, and refer back to them whenever you need to.

In this and following chapters we are going to look at how these basic writing skills go to work—at work—and examine the various forms of written communication that you might have to produce as an office worker.

6.1 Letters

When you first start to work in an organisation's office, it is very unlikely that you will have the responsibility for writing letters, or even for sending memos (memoranda). However, if you want to advance to a more responsible position you will need to know how to handle these forms of communication.

Since we are dealing with business communication, we shall assume that all letters and memos are to be produced on paper that is already headed with the firm's name and address, or, in the case of the memo, with the appropriate heading, which we shall see in Section 6.2.

The types of letter
There are at least six different types of business letter. These are:
(a) letters asking for information **(enquiry)**
(b) letters giving information **(quotation)**
(c) letters expressing anxiety or dissatisfaction **(complaint)**
(d) letters dealing with the complaints of others **(adjustment)**
(e) letters giving a **reference** at the request of a prospective employer
(f) a **circular** letter for distribution in a small area of a town or city, usually for advertising purposes.

The general layout of letters

Broadly speaking, letters should be thought of as having three parts: a beginning, a middle and an end. The following diagram shows the proposed layout:

Ref Nos

Date

Name and address of recipient

Greeting

<u>Subject Title</u>

1st Section - may be only one sentence to introduce the subject and/or acknowledge any previous letter(s) received.

2nd Section - presents the details in a logical and developing progression. May be several paragraphs. If so, can be numbered to make easy reference.

3rd Section - a conclusion which may be a request for some action to be taken or which simply brings the letter to a close.

Complimentary close

Signature

(Position in firm)

Encs (Enclosures, if any)

Letter of enquiry

Your Ref   Date
Our Ref   BS/bg

Wholesale Floorcoverings
21-23 Frodsham Street
MAINTOWN

Dear Sir

<u>Carpeting Ref No C/234/2</u>

    One of our customers has enquired about the possibility of
obtaining a carpet shown in your advertisement in the 'Daily Gazette'
listed under the reference number of C/234/2.

    We would be glad of further information about the possible supply
of this carpeting, together with trade price, trade discounts, date of
delivery, and any other information which may be of use to us and our
customer.

    Although there is no particular urgency about this situation we
would be glad of your early reply.

        Yours faithfully

Bruce Sailes

Manager
for Blakely Barnes & Co Ltd

Letter of quotation

```
Your Ref   BS/bg
Our Ref    PSK/WR/3


Date


Mr B Sailes
Blakely Barnes & Co Ltd
The Carpet Shop
43 Archway Road
BROADHAM


Dear Mr Sailes

Carpet No C/234/2

Thank you for your letter enquiring about carpeting Cat No C/234/2.
I am pleased to tell you that this is readily available, and that we
shall be pleased to supply whatever your customer requires.

I enclose a leaflet showing our trade prices; trade discounts are 7½%
for payment within seven days, and 5% if accounts are settled within a
month.  Delivery can be made on the day after receipt of your firm
order, and if there is any urgency, we would be glad to arrange delivery
on your telephoned request.

Since this is the first time you have contacted us, we would also be
glad to arrange for our representative to call and see you with our
latest catalogues, together with our very attractive display material,
and samples of carpeting which we are sure would be of interest to your
customers.

We hope to hear from you in the near future and can assure you of
excellent service and supply.

Yours sincerely


Peter S. Kingston


Sales Manager


Enc
```

Before going on to study other types of letter there are a few
points that are worth noting about the above.

(a) You may have noticed that the above letters are presented in
different ways. The first one puts the date on the right-hand
side, uses indented paragraphs (which means starting an
inch or so in from the left margin) and centres the

complimentary close (Yours faithfully) together with the signature. This is called the *semi-indented* style.

The reply puts everything on the left-hand side. This is the *fully blocked* style. It is becoming more and more popular as it saves the time of the typist or word-processor operator who would otherwise have to ensure the alignment of the paragraphs and the centralisation of the complimentary close.

The first letter begins 'Dear Sir', and so closes with 'Yours faithfully'; the second letter begins by addressing the correspondent by name, and therefore ends 'Yours sincerely'.

(b) Notice also the *tone* of the reply. Clearly, the writer wishes to establish a good business relationship with the writer of the letter of enquiry. First, he uses the writer's *name;* he then gives the information asked for, and adds the offer of the visit by a representative to try and promote further business. The whole tone of the letter is intended to promote that very important factor in business called 'goodwill'. He further suggests that the firm would be prepared to supply the carpeting immediately on a 'telephoned request', which may be a business risk, but one that the writer obviously thinks is worth taking.

(c) Note also the difference between trade price and trade discount. Trade price is what the *wholesaler* charges the *retailer*. It has nothing to do with the customer. Trade discount concerns the payment of the bill. If it is paid quickly it attracts certain allowances. These trade discounts, or some part of them, may be passed on to the customer, and on many invoices it clearly states that early payment of the account will give the customer a certain percentage reduction, though not necessarily the same as that allowed by the wholesaler to the retailer.

The letter of complaint

Before we look at an example or two of this type of letter, we should distinguish between letters of complaint sent by customers or clients, which are usually about unsatisfactory goods or services, and letters of complaint sent by firms, which are usually about the non-payment of bills and accounts. The important point to remember is that firms do not normally wish to lose customers or clients, therefore the letters of complaint need to be composed with as much tact and thoughtfulness as possible. We shall look, to start with, at the type of *first* letter that a firm may send to a customer who has not, according to the firm's records, kept up with payments or paid a bill.

```
Our Ref    BS/bg
Your Ref
```

```
Date
```

```
Mrs F Johnson
3 Addison Walk
BROADHAM
```

```
Dear Mrs Johnson
```

Account Number 2375643

```
Our records show that we have received no payment from you for the past
three months for the carpeting you bought last July.
```

```
If circumstances have arisen which have caused you difficulty in main-
taining the payments you agreed to make, please do not hesitate to let
us know.  Perhaps we can come to some alternative arrangement for payment.
```

```
If you would telephone the firm, or call personally, I would be glad to
discuss the matter with you and am sure we could come to some arrangement
which would be satisfactory to us both.
```

```
Yours sincerely
```

Bruce Sailer

```
Manager
```

Again, there are a few special points to note about this type of letter of complaint from a firm to a customer

(a) Perhaps the most important point concerns the *tone* of the letter, which is the result of two assumptions: (i) that the firm wishes to keep the customer, and (ii) that this is the *first* letter to remind the customer of the failure to pay. The tone is therefore friendly and understanding, in that it recognises that most customers expect to have to pay for their purchases and that, therefore, there are probably good reasons why such payment has not been made. For example, the customer may not have received the invoice reminding her that the payment is due; she may have sent a cheque or postal order that the firm has not yet received (many first reminders like the above add that 'if payment has been made before receiving this, please ignore this letter'); she may temporarily be short of money or illness or other domestic circumstances may have prevented her from fulfilling her obligations.

Whatever the reason may be, the firm is giving the customer both an inoffensive reminder and an invitation to explain.

(b) Notice that the letter is signed by the Manager. Any senior officer may sign such a letter, as it then makes clear to the customer that this is not merely a routine letter sent out by an accounts clerk, and that the suggestion of a personal interview is from a high level of management.

(c) The third point is the use of two reference titles. One is the filing reference used by the firm and usually consists of the initials of the person dictating the letter, followed by the initials of the typist or word-processor operator, and this appears at the top left of the letter. The other is the account number, which is another way of identifying the customer fairly rapidly if she replies by letter. This is usually placed in the centre of the letter (or on the left if the letter is fully blocked) on the line *below* the greeting. It is normally underlined, but no punctuation is used. The use of 'Your ref:' is only for correspondence with other firms who would also have some sort of filing system; private individuals would have no reference.

Further letters of complaint

What happens if the customer fails to reply to this first letter or reminder? Any further letters that have to be sent to non-paying customers will, naturally, be rather firmer in tone. Pehaps the second, and even the third letter may be similar to the one above in tone and in offers to help, but the time may come when a stronger line needs to be taken.

Omitting the headings and greeting, and looking only at the contents of such a letter, a customer may well receive something like the following:

```
Our records show that in spite of repeated requests for payment of your
account you seem to have made no reply.  We regret that under the cir-
cumstances we have no alternative but to put this matter into the hands
of our legal representatives, who are instructed to institute proceedings
for the recovery of the amount owing unless we receive some payment from
you within the next seven days.
```

Customer complaints

Whenever a person wishes to complain, it is usually because that person is angry or upset in some way. The first thing to remember therefore is *to wait* at least 24 hours before writing the letter. This cooling off period should enable the person to write in a more reasonable way, and not simply to 'let off steam' by expressing his or her emotions.

There are several points worth noting:

(a) Try to avoid the word 'complaint'. The word may make the recipient react negatively especially if your complaint is unjustified.

(b) Stick to the plain and simple facts.

(c) Do not accuse an organisation of deliberately trying to send you faulty goods or provide a poor service.

(d) Remember that whatever has happened may not be the fault of the company at all. Faulty goods, for instance, may be the result of damage caused in transit; poor service may be because of a breakdown in communications or may even be your own fault because you have given a wrong, incomplete, or misleading address.

It is far better to use phrases such as 'I have not received . . .' than 'You have not sent . . .', and in a first letter of complaint *never* threaten legal action.

Letters of adjustment

Medium- to large-sized companies usually have a department or section whose job it is to deal with all complaints from customers or clients.

Replies depend on the answers to three questions.

(a) Is the firm to blame?

(b) Is the customer or client at fault?

(c) Is there no evidence or proof as to whom is to blame?

(a) If the firm is to blame, there is only one course of action. If faulty goods have been supplied as a result of the firm's negligence, they must be replaced or an offer of a money refund must be made, together with an apology.

(b) If the customer is at fault, it requires a very tactful letter from the firm to explain this. No apology is made, of course, and no responsibility is accepted by the firm.

These letters are probably more acceptable to the customer if signed by a senior partner or official, as this implies that his 'complaint' has been taken seriously and, moreover, that he is not being 'put in his place' by a junior member of staff.

(c)   When there is no proof as to whether the blame attaches to the firm or the customer, most good, reputable organisations, while making no apology, will offer to replace the goods or make a money refund if they wish to retain the goodwill of the customer, or perhaps will suggest some compromise that could be acceptable to them both.

The following are examples of the three types of letter of adjustment outlined above:

(a)   *When the company is at fault*

Thank you for your letter dated .... in which you tell us that the garments we forwarded to you are totally unsuitable as they are all in the wrong size.

We have checked with your Order (No ....) and find that an unusual mistake has been made by our packing department, which is normally very reliable and accurate. We have already despatched a parcel to you with the goods in the correct sizes, and hope that you will accept our apologies for any inconvenience this error may have caused.

If you kindly return the original garments we would be most grateful, and have included in the despatched parcel postage stamps which will cover the cost of postage.

Yours sincerely

(b)   *When the customer is at fault*

Thank you for your letter dated .... in which you point out that we have apparently charged you £135.70 more than the goods you ordered this month.

I immediately checked your account, and saw that this amount was the balance owing on last month's statement, and has therefore been included in the current account. I enclose a photocopy of the relevant entry in our ledger for your inspection.

I realise that this additional amount may cause you a problem, so please do not hesitate to call in and ask for me personally, or telephone (Extension 333). I am sure we can come to some mutually satisfactory arrangement for payment.

Yours sincerely

Kenneth Exton.

Executive Sales Manager

Note the attempt to avoid making the customer feel foolish and the use of 'I investigated immediately . . .'. This implies the serious view taken of the complaint, and also the 'personal' approach of the Manager, who is prepared to negotiate payment, and who also wants to ensure as far as possible that the customer continues to use the firm.

(c)   *When there is no proof who is at fault*

We were very sorry to learn from your letter dated .... that the goods you ordered have not arrived.

An immediate enquiry was made at our warehouse, and the records show that the goods were dispatched to you on .... We are making every enquiry at this end from British Rail, who were to carry the goods, and suggest that you might also make enquiries at your nearest parcels depot.

Meanwhile, as we understand your disappointment, our Warehouse Manager has been asked to send another consignment to you, which you should receive within a day or so.

If the original order should turn up, we would be grateful if you would let us know, and we will make arrangements for collection at a time convenient to you.

Yours sincerely

Georgina Forbes (Mrs)

Manager

Clearly, this is no admission of responsibility, but a simple statement of the fact that the goods were sent. Not every organisation would offer to replace the goods, but it would certainly help the goodwill between customer and firm, and many organisations take the view that to risk a loss of the value of the goods is better than losing a customer. In this example, the firm does not send a copy of the warehouse despatch records, but many firms would, as evidence of their having fulfilled their part of the contract.

The other two types of business letter are the **circular** and the **reference**. These are dealt with on pages 37 and 115 respectively.

6.2   Memos

The *memorandum* (memo for short) is simply a letter to someone *inside* your company. Consequently, it should be properly laid out (usually on a printed form) and should have a beginning, a middle and an end. It should also be written in good English, in complete sentences and paragraphed appropriately.

There are, however, at least two important differences between an ordinary letter and a memo:

1   Memos never begin with a *greeting,* such as 'Dear Sir', or 'Dear George', and *never* end with 'Yours faithfully' or 'sincerely'.

2   Quite often, memos are not signed, but initialled, as the name of the sender usually appears at the top. However, if a 'status' or 'position' (i.e. General Manager, Secretary etc.) is used in the heading, it is advisable to sign the memo just like any other letter.

Note: Speaking of signatures, it is less confusing to recipients if you sign your full name, as then they have an indication of your gender. Signatures should also be readable. Printing your name underneath your signature is not necessary if your name can be read easily.

A married woman may add (Mrs) after her name is she wishes to be addressed in that way. Men should *never* sign 'Mr' before or after their name. 'Mr' is a *courtesy title* (unlike 'Mrs', which is a 'married status' title) and is therefore used only by other people when addressing a man.

One final point about signatures: if signing on behalf of a firm or company, it is quite sufficient to write 'for ABC company limited'. The use of 'per' (Latin for 'for') is now regarded as out of date, and the use of 'p.p.' (which means 'per procurationem') carries a certain legal significance and is therefore best avoided.

Example of standard memo heading

M E M O R A N D U M

To: Date:

From: Subject:

(**Note**: The four items above can be arranged in any order. Remember that there is *no greeting,* and that the memo does *not* have a *complimentary close*.)

6.3   Writing Reports

Sooner or later, in most occupations, and particularly in secretarial and clerical work, we are called upon to write a report.

A report can be made for one of two reasons: either you have been asked to make it, or you have information that you think should be passed on to someone in authority.

Whichever kind of report is written, there are certain basic guidelines that should be followed.

(a) A report should always have a *title* that expresses briefly what it is about. This is for the convenience of whoever has to deal with it.

(b) It should be clearly divided between *fact* and *opinion*.

(c) It should be written in good English and in complete sentences, unless you have been requested to write it in 'note-form'.

(d) It should be *practical;* which means that if you make any suggestions or recommendations, they should be able to be acted upon.

(e) It should follow a *pattern* or *layout,* examples of which are given below.

(f) It should always be *signed* and *dated*. The signature is necessary to show who has written the report, and the date is essential as sometimes reports are not read until considerable time has elapsed.

Many reports can be submitted on a standard printed form, such as an *accident* report form.

The informal report

Title (Report on ....)

1st section - a statement of the FACTS usually beginning with the date time and place of whatever is being reported.

2nd section - what your OPINIONS are about the incident, together with any suggestions or recommendations if they are required, and if they would be useful and practical.

Signature

Position in firm or organisation

Date

It is sometimes difficult to decide exactly what kind of report to use, so the best guideline is to ask: for whom is the report intended? If it is for your immediate superior—a supervisor or manager—we can use an *informal* report. If, on the other hand, you know that the report is to go up to the Board of Directors or the Chairman of the Company or to a local council, then a *formal* report is called for.

The differences between the two are quite straightforward. The *informal report* is written in *two* sections; the *formal report* is written in *five* sections. Here is an example of an informal report.

<u>Report On Accident To Word-Processor</u>

On 3 May 19XX at 2.30 in the afternoon, a word-processor was damaged in the accounts department.

An office junior, William Jackson, was hurrying to deliver an urgent message to the Chief Clerk, and was therefore running between the rows of desks in the Accounts Office. He slipped and in falling pushed a word-processor monitor off the desk on which Miss Walters was working. The monitor fell to the floor and was subsequently found to be damaged. The damage has been assessed by the maintenance staff, who say that it cannot be repaired and that a new monitor will be required.

William was apparently unhurt and continued on his way to deliver the message, but it is thought that his fall was caused by the state of the floor, which was highly polished. Our cleaners are excellent in their servicing of the departments, but the type of polish used is to be questioned.

It is suggested that an alternative non-slip polish be found for the cleaning staff's use, and that the monitor be replaced as soon as possible. Since it would appear that no blame attaches to our office junior, it is also suggested that no disciplinary action be taken against him.

                              Supervisor

3 May 19XX

It will be noticed from the above example that there is a careful division between *fact* and *opinion*.

The formal report
Here we are dealing with the kind of report that is submitted to a much higher level of management. The report is divided into *five* sections, which should be memorised as follows:

<u>Title</u> (Report on ....)

Terms of Reference

Reports of this kind are usually requested by management. They are usually referred to as investigation reports and should begin with a statement of what instructions were initially received. These instructions should have been given in writing and should state clearly the required area of investigation. The report therefore begins with a statement of what the limits of the investigation are, the name of the person who gave the instructions for the investigation and possibly (if stated in the instructions) the date by which the report should be made. 'Terms of reference' means, therefore, 'What I have been told to do, and by whom'.

Proceedings

The second section is simply a list of actions taken, with appropriate dates, in order to find out the FACTS. This may include interviews, consultations, use of books, catalogues and any other sources of information relevant to the report. NO INFORMATION should be given at this point in the report.

Findings

These are the FACTS which have been discovered; this section will perhaps be the largest part of the report.

It is important to express here ONLY the FACTS. No opinions should be allowed to creep in – not even other people's opinions – and it is important to arrange the material in a clear and logical order. To assist the reader it is often useful to NUMBER the points raised – a method which can also be followed in all the following sections.

Conclusions

This is the place for OPINIONS. Several people may have expressed opinions, and they may be included here. They must not be taken as FACTS unless there is no doubt that what they say can be substantiated.

Recommendations

As was stated earlier, these should always be PRACTICAL. It is no use recommending actions which are impossible for the firm or organisation to undertake. In some investigations, no recommendations are required; in others the recommendations are of greatest importance, so must be arranged logically, clearly, and preferably be numbered.

SIGNATURE

Date

If the report outlined above is for the highest levels of management, such as a board of directors or a local council, then the *headings* should be used.

However, there are two other ways of presenting such a report—one is by *letter,* the other is by *memo.* In these cases, while the five-section pattern should be followed, the headings will *not* be used. In the case of the letter, the normal greeting and complimentary close are used; in the case of the memo, no greeting is used, there is no complimentary close, and if your name appears in the heading, you would simply *initial* the document.

Sometimes it is necessary to include some technical details, such as statistics, a map or drawing, graphs or charts, etc. In such cases, while they properly belong to the *Findings* section, it is probably better to attach these to the report on a separate sheet or sheets of paper, and ask the reader to refer to them as part of the Findings section.

Reports are invariably written in the *past tense.* This means that if you have to report a speech or some comment made to you, you have to turn these into *reported* or *indirect* speech. We shall be looking at this in some detail in Chapter 7.

6.4   Creative Writing

From our brief look at report writing it should have become clear that the most important factor is arranging material in a logical and orderly fashion. In the case of a report we have a two- or five-section plan to follow.

When writing an article, an essay or brochure material, we also need a clear *plan.* There are certain guidelines that you may find useful in the preparation of any rather lengthy piece of writing.

(a) First write down all your thoughts on the chosen subject. Do not worry at this stage about putting them in any particular order. You should aim at about fifteen or twenty *different* ideas or statements. The twin perils of writing are *repetition* and *irrelevance.* You must check carefully, therefore, that you are not repeating an idea in a slightly different form and that all the ideas relate to your theme or subject.

(b) The next step is to look carefully through the list of ideas and *group together* those ideas that are very closely related. This may well reduce your original list of statements to six or seven.

(c) It is necessary now to arrange these ideas in a logical and orderly progression, so that the reader may follow your line of thought or argument easily. Having grouped the ideas together, *number* them so that they follow a developing progression of thought.

(d) The most difficult part of composition is knowing how to start and how to end; this is because the reader will get the strongest impressions from the start and the finish. In other words, the opening and the concluding paragraphs need very careful attention.

(e) Clearly, the sort of language you use has to be pitched to the kind of audience you expect and should be appropriate to the subject. You would not, for example, use the same language or choice of words for fairly young children as you would for their parents. Equally, you would not write about a market in the same way you would write about a cathedral or a serious accident.

6.5 Telexes and Telephone Messages

However *written* work in an office is produced, it should be expressed in good English, which means that it should be written in *complete*, grammatically correct and properly punctuated sentences. In addition, of course, it should be set out in a logical and orderly manner, neatly, clearly, and in understandable language appropriate to the reader.

However, there are occasions when we have to try and compress or contract what we want to say into as short and concise a form as possible. One such occasion is when we wish to transmit information by *telex* using a *teleprinter*. This service extends to many countries throughout the world, so that messages may be transmitted to almost anywhere on the globe. The transmission is paid for by the *time taken*, therefore it is to a firm's advantage to see that the messages are as brief as possible but not lacking any detail, and that a high-speed typist is employed to send them.

The important thing is to make the message as brief as possible and yet include all the essential details. In other words, we have to be able to *summarise*. This involves rather special skills, so we shall be looking at this in detail later.

But first, let us look at an example of a *telex* message, beginning with the *full text* (see page 82).

Not including the letter heading, the signature, and the name and address of the recipient, there are about 90 words in this letter. A corresponding *telex* message must be brief but contain all the relevant details.

Firm's Letter Heading

Date

Name and address of the recipient

Dear Sir

There is to be a full meeting of the Management Board on Tuesday the
2nd of next month (May) at which your attendance would be appreciated.

It would also be appreciated if you would bring your files and records
concerning the B22/C and CTS/34 projects, as these will be the main
items of discussion.

If you find there are any difficulties about attending, or find it
necessary to nominate someone to appear in your place, please notify
me as soon as possible.

Yours faithfully

CHAIRMAN

It will help if we make a list of these 'relevant details' in the
following manner:

1   Date of meeting
2   Files required
3   Name of deputy

Now we can write out the message for transmission by the
teleprinter operator. It should look something like this:

Firm's directory no

MANDIR   Board meets Tuesday 2 May.   Files B22/C CTS/34 required.
Please notify name of possible deputy asap.

Chairman

There are two things to notice when the letter is reduced to only
thirteen words:
(a) Brevity does not abandon politeness, so 'please' is still
    included.
(b) The use of 'asap' is standard in office language and means

'as soon as possible'. This is also used in brief memos or notes of telephone messages, but not in letters or other documents. The contraction of 'Managing Director' to *mandir* will also be understood by the recipient.

The same system of contraction is used for noting telephone or verbal messages. It is probably better to note down *more* than is actually required, taking particular care over names, addresses, account numbers and so on, and then to write out the message as briefly as possible.

6.6   Summarising

Of course, it is not only telex messages that have to be as brief as possible. There are many other occasions when we may be required to summarise.

The method described below is useful and effective but is not the only method.

First, the material we have to summarise should be read *carefully* so that we know exactly what it is about. We need to know the *main theme*, as this is going to be an important measure of what we should include and what we should leave out. This main theme should then be noted down—preferably in one sentence. This will be useful as a *title* for the summary, as all summaries should have a title.

The second step is to go through the document paragraph by paragraph and *eliminate* any paragraph that is not essential and relevant to the main theme. In a document of, say, ten paragraphs, we may be able to leave out two or three—particularly the first and possibly the second. Do not assume that summarising means that every paragraph must be contracted. Material should only be retained if it is *essential* and *relevant* to the main theme.

The third step is to find the *main sentences* in each essential and relevant paragraph. These should be noted down; you should then have a list of several sentences that are the main points of the document. It is useful to leave a few lines between each noted sentence, for important details to be filled in later.

Main sentences should be placed either at the *beginning* or at the *end* of a paragraph (see Section 7.1) so concentrate on these places to find out the main sentence in each relevant paragraph.

The final step in this preparation process is now to read each paragraph carefully for important *details*. These should be noted between each main sentence.

We now have a pattern that looks like this:

```
Title (the sentence summarising the general theme)

1  Main sentence in first relevant and essential paragraph

   (a)  detail

   (b)  detail

2  Main sentence

   (a)  detail

   (b)  detail

3  Main sentence

   (a)  detail

   (b)  detail

   (c)  detail

                        etc etc
```

Writing the summary

Once the preparation stage has been completed thoroughly, and we have checked and rechecked to be sure that everything essential has been included, we are ready to write the summary in a concise yet readable form.

Consider the following points when writing the summary:

1   It must be written in complete sentences, correctly constructed and punctuated. (The exception to this rule is when you are specifically asked—as in some examination papers—to present the summary in note-form.)

2   It need not follow the exact pattern of the original document's 'idea order', i.e. you can move paragraphs about if you think that it will be easier for the reader to follow.

3   It must be written in the language, style and tone that will suit the reader. Technical or scientific terms should only be used if the reader will be familiar with them, otherwise they should be explained. However, in a summary there is little scope for long explanations.

4   It must be edited and 'pruned' to make sure that no unnecessary words have been used, and that groups of nouns or adjectives have been replaced by single substitutes.

For example, if the original refers to 'engineers, body-repairers, fitters, tyre-replacers, car electricians, and spare-parts suppliers . . .' all these *nouns* can be replaced by *motor mechanics* or *car maintenance staff*. Similarly, if the original reference was to the 'brown, green, yellow, red, ochre, scarlet, and russet leaves of Autumn . . .' these *adjectives* can be replaced by *multi-coloured*.

5   Figures of speech such as metaphors and similes should not be included in summaries, however interesting and arresting they may be. Also, *statistics*, unless essential to the summary, should be either omitted or condensed into a general statement. For example, if the original states that 'in 1976 X% of workers in banks were men, but by 1987 Y% were women workers' we could express this more concisely by writing 'By 1987 there were 2% more women than men in banks' or, even more simply: 'There are more women than men in banking'. The point about statistics is whether the figures are essential to what the writer is wanting to say. If they are, then they must be included in full; if not, then they can be condensed.

Let us look at an example of a script that has to be summarised:

Middle Management

In answer to the question: What is middle management? it can be said that first, IT IS A POSITION OF AUTHORITY.

This causes some people to rush into a managerial post, if given the opportunity, without reflecting on what is involved. It is one thing to have power and authority over other people; it is quite another thing to be able to handle that power and authority in such a way as to secure maximum co-operation between colleagues and staff, and to be able to secure really effective communication not only with seniors, but also with junior staff.

Secondly, it is A POSITION OF RESPONSIBILITY. The responsibilities range over a wide area. But what do these responsibilities involve? In the first place the manager is liable to be called to account by senior management for any problems which may arise; he is answerable for any situations likely to cause embarrassment to the company by anything which happens in his department, and he is morally accountable for the behaviour of his staff as it affects the work situation and production. He must also create good credit and a reputable character rating, and be known as reliable and trustworthy, both to seniors and juniors. Clearly, responsibility is not only the matter of discharging duties, but is is also concerned with the personal integrity of the manager, and with the standards he sets for himself.

(The above is a short extract from the author's book *It's My Business to Know!* published by McGraw-Hill.)

Having read the extract carefully once or twice, we can begin to analyse it in the manner suggested above.

Although the title given is *Middle Management*, this would not be adequate or accurate enough for the summary of this little extract. In the first place, we are summarising only *two* paragraphs, and therefore the title needs to identify only these two. In the second place, such a title would be too vague. The two paragraphs are concerned with two aspects of middle management, not the whole subject, therefore we must think of a title that describes the extract *as exactly as possible*. For example, it would be far more accurate to describe it as 'two aspects of middle management' or 'the first two points a middle manager must consider'. (You may be able to think of better titles than these.) The *accuracy* of the title is more important than the *length*. One- or two-word titles may seem attractive but in practice they are of little value if they are too *vague*.

We now write down the title of the document:

'The first two points a middle manager must consider.'

Now we have to find the *main sentences*. Clearly there are *two*.

1 Middle Management is a position of authority.

2 It carries responsibilities.

If we write these down, leaving a gap between them, we are now ready to add the *details*, so that we complete a structure that looks like this:

The first two points a Middle Manager must consider

1 Position of authority

(a) Use of authority must secure maximum co-operation between staff

(b) Must also ensure good communication both upwards and downwards

2 Responsibilities

(a) Has to answer to senior staff for actions in his section

(b) Must be respected and trusted and set standards for himself

From these notes you can now write a summary of the original extract. Write the summary entirely from your notes, returning to the original only to check that all the essential points have been included. You should complete the summary in no more than 70 words, which is roughly one-third the length of the original text.

Although a summary may be of any length, providing it is shorter than the original, it is a good guide to work to the standard of one-third the length of the original. This is technically called a *précis* and is what is normally required in an English examination.

The test of a good summary is that the reader should not be able to tell it is a summary. It should flow smoothly, contain enough material to be clear and be correctly punctuated. Many summaries can be written in one paragraph, though in the example given above, there is a natural division into two. (See Section 7.1 on 'Paragraphs'.)

6.7   Writing for the Reader

Unless you know the reader you should write in the same way as you would for a *general* reader. In other words, your language should be *easily understandable* and you should avoid using any technical or scientific phrases or long and unfamiliar words that could confuse.

Jargon is the word used to describe the language we use from day to day in the profession we are employed in. (See also Chapter 2.) It is familiar to those who work with us, but its meaning is often a mystery to anyone outside the organisation.

One of the first things we have to learn when we start work, is the 'language' of the workplace or, in the case of a student starting college, the equally mysterious codes that identify the courses. It is much easier for staff and students alike to refer to a course as 'PSC2', but it is almost impossible for an outsider to interpret that as the second year of a part-time secretarial course.

Never use jargon when communicating with people outside your office or course. The Golden Rule is *always to write clearly and understandably,* using only language which most people with an average education can follow without difficulty.

Questions

1 Name six of the commonest types of business letter and the purposes for which they are used.
2 If a firm receives a letter of complaint, what three questions should be asked before any reply is attempted?
3 Describe the difference between a semi-indented and fully blocked presentation of a business letter.
4 It is stated earlier that a letter should have 'a beginning, a middle and an end'. What should these three sections consist of?

5 'I recently purchased a lawnmower from your firm, which, alas, now fails to work and I am very disappointed.'
   The above sentence, part of a letter of complaint, contains at least one of each of the eight *parts of speech*. Try to identify these parts of speech. Only one example of each need be stated. Can you also identify a serious *ambiguity* in the construction of the sentence, and suggest an alternative way of writing this sentence to avoid this error?
6 There are two main types of report. Describe each of them briefly.
7 A piece of office equipment is not working properly. Write an *informal report* to your supervisor describing the problem and what you think may be the cause. You can choose any piece of equipment with which you are familiar. The report should be presented in the form of a *memorandum*.
8 You have been given a pamphlet that contains new regulations concerning Health and Safety at Work, and have been asked by your employer to summarise it. Describe the step-by-step *method* you could use to do this.

Chapter 7

More English at Work

In this chapter we shall be looking first at the construction of paragraphs, then at how to write reported speech, with a brief reference to writing direct speech, and finally at the wording of staff notices and announcements.

7.1 Paragraphs

We noted earlier that a sentence should contain only *one* idea. This is also the case with a paragraph. Whether the paragraph is only one sentence or dozens of sentences the rule is that it must *only* contain *one* basic *idea*. As soon as you introduce a different idea, you must start a new paragraph!

As a paragraph should contain only one idea, it follows that this idea will be expressed in one sentence. The rest of the paragraph will be an extension or development of this idea.

This *main* or *topic* sentence should either start the paragraph or end it. Write it elsewhere and it will not 'register' in the mind of the reader as effectively.

These alternative constructions of a paragraph are given special names. If the main or topic sentence is placed at the beginning, it is a *loose* construction; if it is left to the end it is a *periodic* construction. These names are not important, but they may act as a reminder to plan the paragraphs deliberately.

Different writers aim for different effects and so favour the paragraph construction that best suits their needs. For instance, an advertising copy-writer is likely to want to grab her reader's attention straight away, so will lead with her topic sentence: 'Recent tests prove that Sudso washes . . .'. A thriller writer, on the other hand, wants to maintain suspense so uses a periodic construction—tucking the corpse away at the end of the paragraph. In general, however, the rest of us should try to use a mixture of loose and periodic paragraph constructions, to give variety to our writing.

7.2   Reported Speech and Direct Speech

In the section on writing reports you were referred to this section. This is because *all* conversation referred to in a report should be written in reported speech.

If you remember that we use reported speech nearly every day whenever we tell anyone what someone else has said, you will realise that writing reported speech is quite a natural and everyday thing. For example, if you were telling one person what someone else had said, you would automatically drop into reported speech. Someone may have said 'I'm going to apply for a clerical post at the XYZ Company today'. When you tell your friend, you would say: 'She said that she was going to apply for a clerical post at the XYZ Company that day.'

You have made *four* changes to the original spoken words.

1   You have used an 'introduction'—she said that . . . .
2   You have changed the verb to the past tense—'am' has become 'was'.
3   You have changed 'today' to 'that day', because the actual words may have been spoken a week or more ago and it would be nonsense to say 'today'.
4   You have changed the personal pronoun 'I' to 'she'.

These, then, are the *four rules* we have to remember when using reported speech—all *verbs* must go *one tense back in time* ('am' becomes 'was', 'was' becomes 'had been', etc.); words denoting the 'present' must go into the 'past', (e.g. 'now' becomes 'then', 'here' becomes 'there', 'tomorrow' becomes 'the next day', etc.); all personal pronouns go into the 'third person', (e.g. 'I' = he or she, 'me' = him or her, 'you' (plural) = they, etc.); and every piece of reported speech begins with an introduction which identifies the speaker, and sometimes the time and place as well.

Although we may not stick exactly to these rules when we are speaking, it is important to remember them when making a report or when taking minutes of a committee meeting.

Here is a brief example to illustrate the way the rules apply. The following passage is direct speech (conversation quoted word for word):

George said, 'I hope to be able to qualify as a clerk in retail and distribution when I take the examinations at the end of this year'.

1   To translate this into reported speech first we introduce the speaker. In this case we do not need to make any changes, and can begin by writing: George said that. . . . Notice that the word 'that' has been added. This is not essential but it is helpful as a reminder that what follows is in reported speech and not in direct speech.

2   The first word inside the quotation marks is 'I'. This has to be changed to the 'third person', in this case 'he'. So now we have 'George said that *he*. . . .'

3   The second word is the verb 'hope'. This must change one tense into the past, so this becomes 'hope*d*'. Similarly, later in the sentence he says 'when I take . . .'. We change the pronoun 'I' to 'he', but the verb is used to imply a *future* occasion, so we bring this back into the present, i.e. 'takes . . .'.

4   He then refers to '. . . this year'. We have to find a word that would apply if the report were made after 'this year' had passed. We could use ' . . . *the* year'.

With these changes we now have:

George said *that he hoped* to be able to qualify as a clerk in Retail and Distribution when *he takes* the examinations at the end of *the* year.

Notice that *no other words are changed*. Often students misunderstand the nature of reported speech and re-write what has been said in their own words. This is *not* reported speech, this is paraphrasing. In reported speech we change only those words indicated in the rules above; all other words remain unaltered. However, there are *two* occasions when the verb is not put into the past tense.

1   When it refers to a state of existence and not an action, for example, George said, 'I broke my leg when I was fourteen'. Normally, 'was' would be changed to 'had been', but the 'was' in this sentence refers to 'being fourteen', which is a state of existence and not an action, so it remains unchanged. Thus, the reported speech would read: George said *that he had broken his* leg when *he was* fourteen.

2   When altering it would change the *meaning* of the sentence, i.e. when the verb refers to a permanent condition or state of

affairs. For example: George said, 'Road signs in Britain are used to help motorists'. If we put 'are' into the past tense (George said that road signs *were* used . . .) this seems to suggest that they are no longer used.

Direct speech
It is not often that we have to write direct speech, that is, quote a conversation word for word, but if we do it is necessary to know how to punctuate it properly.

At first sight the punctuation of direct speech seems to be very complicated. However, it is relatively simple once certain rules or principles are understood.

1   All direct speech is enclosed in inverted commas. These are marks that *separate* the spoken words from any unspoken words in the same sentence. For example, George said, ''........,'' when he spoke at the meeting. In the example *double inverted commas* have been used, and traditionally these are used, especially in hand-written documents. However, *single speech marks* are preferable in printed material as double speech marks tend to give a rather heavy or cluttered appearance to the page.

There are occasions, however, when the double quotes are essential, and these are when there is a 'quotation within a quotation' as, for example: 'Why did she shout ''help!'',' he asked, 'when she wasn't in danger?'

2   Direct speech may be introduced by a *comma,* though in the past it was considered necessary to use a *colon* before the spoken words began.

3   There are *three* ways of setting out direct speech:
    (a) by an introductory phrase, for example, George said, 'I shall be going to town this afternoon to buy a shirt';
    (b) by 'splitting' the spoken words with the unspoken words, for example, 'I shall be going to town this afternoon,' George said, 'to buy a shirt';
    (c) by putting the unspoken words at the end of the sentence, for example, 'I shall be going to town this afternoon to buy a shirt,' George said.

You need to study carefully the position of the commas and full-stops in the above examples; the full-stop in each case *ends the sentence* that includes the unspoken words as well as the spoken ones and is placed *outside* the final speech mark.

If the sentence contains no unspoken words (for example, 'I am going to town this afternoon to buy a shirt.') the full-stop is placed *after the last word* and *inside* the final speech mark.

4   If you have to write a conversation between two or more people, and if it is a fairly lengthy one, the simplest way of setting it out is in *play-form*. The names of the speakers are put on the left and the spoken words put alongside, without speech marks.

For example:

George: I think I'll go to town this afternoon to buy a shirt.
Jack: Don't forget you have an appointment with the dentist.
George: What a good job you reminded me! I'd completely forgotten!
Jill: Perhaps we could meet in town later—if you're feeling O.K.
George: Good idea! I should be all right. It's only an inspection.

As you will see, this is a much simpler form than writing George said, Jack said, and so on, and using quotation marks, but it is not often appropriate to the subject matter.

7.3   Writing Notices and Announcements

Communication within an office often depends on the use of notices and announcements that are either posted on notice boards or, if the notice is regarded as especially important, delivered to each member of the staff separately.

Great care should be taken with the wording of such notices.

The first point to remember is the importance of *avoiding any suggestion of discrimination*. By discrimination we mean giving any impression that one group or individual is preferred to another. There are three major areas of possible discrimination:

(a) sexual discrimination, where men seem to be preferred to women, or vice versa;

(b) racial discrimination, where a particular racial group seems to be preferred over another;

(c) social discrimination, where one person or group is preferred to another because of class differences or advantages, such as attending a certain school or belonging to a certain club.

The second point to remember is the danger of *ambiguity*. Make sure that what you write cannot be interpreted in more than one way. For example, a notice or advertisement that says:

'WANTED—a basket for a puppy with handles at each
side and a waterproof bottom'

may cause a lot of smiles, but does not give a very good impression
of the intelligence of the writer.

The third point concerns *language*. Not only must any suggestion
of discrimination, and any ambiguity be avoided, but what we
have to say must be *understandable* to all who may read the notice.

For example, it would be perfectly correct to write:

'Scintillate, scintillate globe vivific
Would I could fathom thy nature specific
Loftily poised in the ether capacious
Strongly resembling a gem carbonaceous!'

but how many people would understand it, without reference to a
dictionary? Yet it is one of the best known of children's rhymes!
Put into its familiar (and therefore *understandable*) form it is:

'Twinkle, twinkle, little star,
How I wonder what you are.
Up above the world so high,
Like a diamond in the sky!'

Clearly, one's choice of language must be made with the *reader* in
mind. Any language that is not readily understandable is a waste of
time and effort.

Questions

1 Study the following groups of words; indicate which are
sentences and which are not, and say why not:
    (a) The birds singing in the trees.
    (b) I live near the river.
    (c) Always say 'No' to drugs!
    (d) Details follow in a moment.
    (e) Three blind mice: see how they run.
    (f) They all run after the farmer's wife.
2 What should a paragraph consist of. Explain two possible kinds
of paragraph you could use.
3 Turn the following extract from a speech into reported speech:
    'I am glad to be here this evening at the annual dinner of the
Students' Union. I have always been interested in the activities
of the SU, and believe that it does a very good job of work. I

think that its support for many sporting and social activities is commendable, but I have always been particularly impressed by the way it has helped students who have not had the money required to pay for examination fees and, sometimes, have been assisted to pay for their lodgings and other expenses. We all know that grants are very inadequate by modern standards and I strongly support the protests and demonstrations organised by the Union – providing, of course, that they are always peaceful and non-violent.'

4 Punctuate the following direct speech:

What are you doing today the Manager asked his secretary I am hoping to finish off the filing she replied then I hope to take an early lunch as I have a lot of work to do this afternoon fine the manager replied I shall be leaving for London this evening so I'd be glad if you would look up some train times for me certainly sir she said will you be away long

(Note: Begin a new line for each speaker.)

5 In the office there has been petty thieving—handbags, pens, a raincoat and other items. Draw up a *notice* for the staff advising them of what measures to take to ensure greater safety for their possessions. Include also instructions as to what should be done if a cheque book and/or credit card is missing.

6 Compose an *announcement* to be put on the staff notice board about the possibility of short-time working, which may have to be introduced because of a shortage of orders.

Chapter 8

Office Communication Systems and Graphics

This chapter introduces those aids to business communication not yet covered in this book. The first section deals with how information may best be passed to staff within an office, the second with how information may be communicated visually.

8.1 Communication Systems

Every business has a communication system of some kind. Some systems work more effectively than others.

The *purpose* of any communication system is to convey and to receive information. Many of the problems in industry and commerce are said to be caused by a breakdown in the communication system. We are going to look at some of the possible reasons for this breakdown, but first let us look at some of the systems that businesses use.

Small businesses
In small businesses, for example a one-owner business employing, say, 20 people or so, there should be few problems of communication, as the employer is in constant touch with his (or her) employees. When problems arise, the employer can discuss the matter with all the staff immediately and a solution can often be found relatively quickly. Such an employer is known as a *sole trader*.

If the business prospers, the employer may want to expand, and may take on a partner or two. Usually the partners invest money in the business and this may lead to more staff, larger premises and the further development of what is by now a *limited company*. (The word 'limited' here means that the partners have a 'limited' or 'restricted' responsibility for any debts or financial problems that

96

may occur. The amount for which each is responsible is usually equivalent to the amount each has invested in the company.)

The management are now less involved with the staff and tend to discuss problems amongst themselves. If the business grows, new branches may be opened, and the distance between staff and management may grow. In national and multi-national organisations the management seems remote from the workforce. Communication must pass down through the different levels and equally should be able to pass from the staff or workforce level upwards to the directors and chairman. There should also be an adequate system of communication between managers. In other words, not only should there be a 'downward' and 'upward' flow of information, but also a 'sideways' flow.

Large businesses
Many large businesses adopt a number of devices to give and receive information.

The house magazine
This is printed by many large organisations as a way of contacting the whole staff. It is usually a 'glossy magazine' issued monthly, containing articles and illustrations of general interest as well as, from time to time, items concerning plans and changes of policy within the company. Some companies charge for the magazine, so, unfortunately, not all the staff see it.

Bulletins or newsletters
These on the other hand, are distributed free of charge to all members of staff, usually weekly. This means that the information is more up to date and that, whether all the staff read it or not, everyone receives a copy. This bulletin or newsletter is often just a typed information sheet, duplicated and distributed with the salary advice or wage packet. Again this gives management the opportunity to set out any changes or proposals likely to affect the staff.

Personal memos
These are sent to every member of staff by name, which means that the recipient is almost guaranteed to read it. Not only is this a great advantage, but opportunity can be given for staff to make some kind of response, either by including a questionnaire or by suggesting a meeting at which various points of view can be aired.

The drawback with this is that it is costly both in money and in time for those who have to prepare and distribute it.

The staff notice-board

Perhaps this is the most commonly used form of written communication within an organisation, but, as anyone who has worked in an office or factory knows, it has considerable drawbacks.

The first of these is that it usually contains all company information in addition to information from management. Consequently, relatively few staff can spend the time necessary to read every document, and items which are of particular interest may well be missed in the clutter.

The second problem is that information usually has to be compressed onto a single sheet of paper. This results in a lack of detail and sometimes in a terse style, which can cause resentment or misunderstanding.

The third problem is that outdated notices tend to be left on the notice-board, so unless documents are carefully dated, and old ones removed, one is never sure how current the information is.

The display board

This is a development of, and an improvement upon, the staff notice-board and is set up in places where staff are most likely to see it and, it is hoped, read it.

The display board information is usually confined to only *one* subject and can be set out attractively to catch the eye of the passer-by. Although only single sheets are used, they may be continuous, and therefore the drawbacks of over-compression mentioned above can be avoided.

The display board also has the advantage of providing staff with an opportunity to comment, either through a questionnaire (the papers being available on an adjacent table) or suggestion box. Of course, this can be done with a staff notice-board but this rarely happens.

Again, the problem is that there is no guarantee that all the employees will read the display board, and although management may claim that that is the fault of the employee—the information is there for those who read it—the human factor should be taken into account in any communication system.

Word of mouth

This is the most common form of communication in an organisation. Information is given either over the internal telephone or simply face-to-face.

Unfortunately, this has several unsatisfactory elements about it as we have seen in earlier chapters; messages can so easily be misinterpreted.

8.2 Communication by Drawings

Perhaps the earliest form of communication was by pictures. We know that ancient civilisations such as the Chinese, the North American Indians and the Greeks relied on drawings for their first languages and traces of those languages are still in use. For example, the Greek letter Δ (delta) is really a drawing of the triangular delta sometimes formed by rivers as they enter the sea.

We still use drawings to communicate information. The best known is probably the road sign, which is used and understood internationally.

In business, drawings are used widely to communicate. Graphs, charts, diagrams and similar drawings are found in most offices and information is often given to the public through this medium. It is important, therefore, for anyone taking up a business career to be familiar with as many forms of visual communication as possible.

The following list of drawings or graphics used in business today includes those most commonly used and therefore, the ones we should be familiar with.

Algorithms (sometimes called flow charts)

These are in very wide use, as they are employed in the designing of computer programs. The diagram on page 100 is a flow chart of a computerised customer order system.

Bar charts (sometimes called 'block charts')

These are used to display information in a form that is a little like a graph. Bar charts are usually either multiple or component.

Multiple bar charts simply show the relationship of 'totals' (i.e. quantities) say, over a period of time. Suppose, for example, we wanted to compare, quickly and easily, the number of girl students with the number of boy students in a secretarial department of a

Flowchart of a computerised customer order system

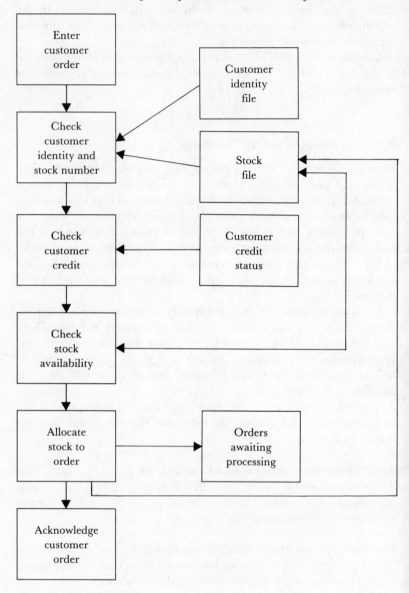

college over a three-year period. The bar chart may look something like this:

Multiple bar chart

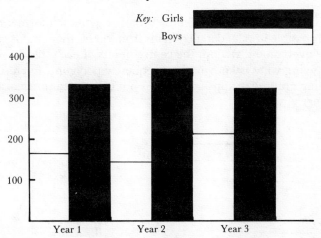

On the other hand, we may need to know more about the actual courses the students were taking. This could be expressed by a component bar chart, which may look like this:

Component bar chart

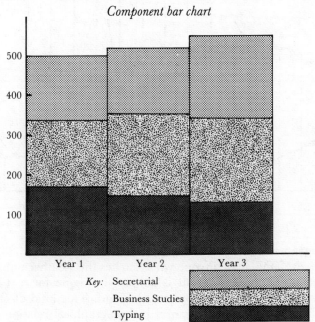

It should be obvious from these examples that in addition to the charts a key or legend must be provided to explain each column. The various markings are meaningless unless such an explanation is given.

Of course, bar charts give only broad or general information. It is not possible to read detailed items from them, though this can be partly overcome if we join the centre points of each 'block' with a line, giving what is known as a 'frequency polygon'. Even so, the resulting graph-like appearance does not give the same accuracy as a proper graph.

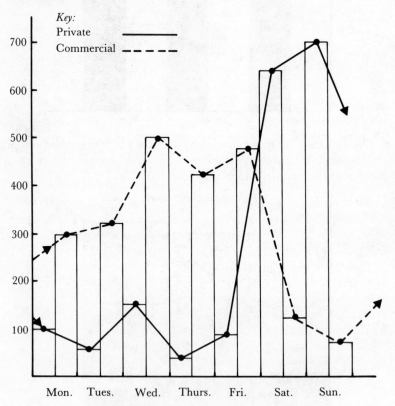

Cartograms

These are familiar to anyone who watches the weather reports on television, as the cartogram is simply the name for a diagram representing a country or an area of land. This kind of chart is useful for showing, for instance, the geographical relation of the branches of a company. It may also be used to convey information to the general public.

Gantt charts

This is a useful way of checking up 'progress made' against 'progress anticipated or forecast', and is widely used by many organisations.

Take, for example, a student who is required to read a number of books each week or month in order to reach a certain standard of knowledge and information. The following diagram shows his progress:

Gantt chart

	Week 1	Week 2	Week 3	Week 4	Week 5
Target	2	2	3	3	3
Achievement	1 ½	2 ½	2	2	4

This chart shows that the student set himself the target of reading 13 books in the five weeks shown. At the end of the fifth week he has read 12, showing a shortfall of one, which will have to be made up.

Graphs

Graphs are drawings most of us learn to read and understand while we are at school, so this section will mention only one or two points worth remembering.

Firstly, graphs may be used to show the rise and fall of a single variable. They may also be used to show *comparisons* between two or more variables. In this case, the relative rise and fall between factors is plotted.

We should try to guard against plotting too many factors on one graph. For example, if we try to represent sales against salaries, the cost of raw materials, the influence of inflation and the changes in the value of the capital assets of a firm on *one* graph, the result will be incomprehensible. The answer to this is to plot only two or three variables on one graph and prepare another graph for the other two or three.

Secondly, we must always consider carefully the *scale* on which we draw our graph. The main purpose of a graph is to deliver *accurate* information. If the scale is too small, we sacrifice accuracy; if it is too large it may give detail but take up an impractical amount of space.

Organisation charts
These are of two kinds: one shows the *structure* of the organisation and the other shows the *function* or type of work done by the members of the organisation.

The first kind should be fairly familiar to most of us. It is sometimes referred to as the *pyramid* or *hierarchy* chart, as it shows how the organisation is structured from the top downwards.

Chairman
|
Board of Directors
|
Departmental Managers
|
Assistant Managers
|
Supervisors
|
Operatives and Workforce

An example of the second kind, which shows the function or duties of the various members, is shown on page 105.

Pictograms
Pictograms are cartoon-type drawings that convey information with the minimum use of words. There is an example of this in the first chapter of this book, where George and Jane are represented trying to communicate over a bar.

Many companies use this kind of 'picture' language as it is easy to 'read' and sometimes amusing; it is a popular method employed in circulars and advertising material.

Pie charts
These look like a pie cut into sections. They show relative quantities. Describing this distribution in words, though sometimes done, is much more difficult—the pie chart shows at a glance the various proportions.

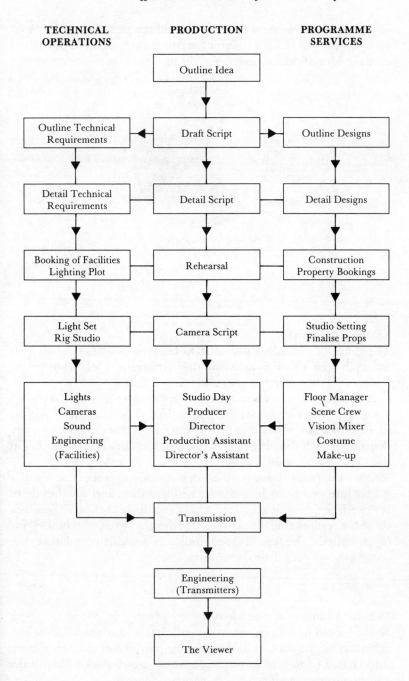

The chart below shows the division of the population of a town according to age. Often different segments are coloured or shaded to make identification easier.

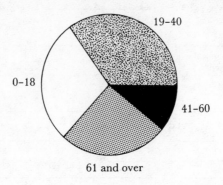

Scatter diagrams
These are of considerable value to businesses as they show, for example, the relation between the performance of branches or outlets and thus provide valuable information.

A retail store may have branches spreading over a wide area. To compare the performance of these outlets, different values may be plotted on a graph (see page 107). Since the scatter diagram is only concerned with showing relative values, it is not necessary to begin the x- or y- scale values at 0.

Once the points have been plotted the management can see at a glance how one branch compares with another, and whether there is a *correlation,* or mutual relation between the branches, or whether there are remarkable differences that then have to be accounted for or explained. The first diagram indicates a strong correlation, the second shows very little correlation.

Tables
We are all aware of the use of tables whether in connection with work, school or college, or to do with bus and train services, etc. They are an important and necessary part of our everyday lives, and enable us to find information much more quickly than if the information were given only in words.

Scatter diagram (a) showing a strong correlation

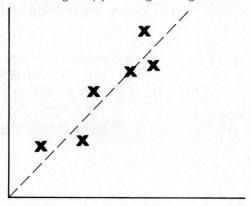

Scatter diagram (b) showing no correlation

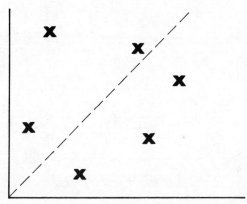

Questions

1 Describe the way the communication system works in your place of employment, or, if you have never been employed, how information is passed on to you at school or college.
2 Prepare a *table* listing the various types of graphs and charts mentioned in the chapter above. This should show the name of the diagram, followed by a brief description of the purpose for which it is used. The table could be set out as follows:

TITLE   PURPOSE

3 You have been asked to analyse the amount of space a certain national newspaper gives to various items. Your results look like

this: current news stories, 15%; sport, 20%; advertising, 56%; articles and reviews, 5%; games, competitions and children's items, 4%.

Draw a *pie chart* to show these proportions. (It would be as well to use a protractor to ensure accuracy, though first, of course, you must work out what each of the above percentages is in degrees, for example, 4% is 4×360 divided by $100 = 14.4$ degrees.)

Chapter 9

'I've Got a Job!'

For many people, these words represent one of the greatest moments in life.

It is important to be able to write good letters of application and present oneself well at an interview if you want a good chance of finding a job. In this chapter we are going to look at these points in some detail, and try to understand why one candidate may be preferred rather than another.

9.1 The Employer's Tasks

Before a job is advertised, the employer has quite a lot of homework to do. He has three major points to consider:
   (a) the preparation of a *job description*
   (b) the drawing up of an *employee specification*
   (c) the setting up of a system to deal with advertising the post, answering replies, and organising interviews.

The preparation of a job description
Every aspect of the duties of the successful candidate must be clearly defined. The following must also be outlined: the hours of work, the working conditions, the question of overtime or work involving unsocial hours, holidays, pay, the opportunities for further training, the team or group with whom the successful candidate will work, and the possibilities of promotion.

This may involve consultation with managers, assistant managers, supervisors and people doing the same or a very similar job as the one to be advertised.

The purpose of this is not only to provide adequate and helpful material for the advertisement, but also to enable an *application form* to be designed, though a general form is often used for this, rather than one referring to a particular post.

109

It is only when this job description has been completed that the employer can form an idea of the kind of person required for the post and so draw up the employee specification.

The employee specification

Obviously, certain jobs require certain kinds of people, sometimes with special physical characteristics. On the other hand, many kinds of employment suit people of any physique, able-bodied or handicapped, and the employer should bear this in mind.

One of the most important elements, if the job entails working with a team or group, is how well the candidate gets on with other people. Also, where the handling of money or confidential papers is involved, how trustworthy and reliable the applicant may be—hence the need for references. The employer may also want to take into account the candidate's home and family background and what outside interests and hobbies they have.

It may seem that the employer is making up his mind beforehand as to just what type of person he wants for a particular post, and this is worth bearing in mind should you be turned down for a job. The reason may well be that you just do not fit the pattern the employer has drawn up. Consequently, you should not feel discouraged or feel there is something wrong with you!

Setting up a system

How should the post be advertised? There are several options available, and an employer may use more than one. The first step the employer usually takes is to inform the whole staff, by means of the staff notice board or the weekly bulletin, that the post is to be advertised. Sometimes, a member of the staff will know of someone who is suited to the post and will inform his or her manager accordingly. A personal recommendation of this kind is usually considered carefully, as an employer often prefers an applicant known to a member of his staff to a complete outsider. This suggests that 'it's not *what* you know but *who* you know', but in fact the selection process is usually very fair; employers are only too anxious to secure the best possible applicant and usually the 'recommended candidate' stands no more chance than the rest.

Finally, the employer has to set up the machinery for coping with replies to the advertisement and the interviews that follow.

First, he has to allocate staff to deal with the replies. In a large firm, the department manager probably has the major responsibility for this, and with a copy of the employer's 'Employee

Specification' (if he has not drawn it up himself) can select from the applicants those who seem suitable for interview. Since there are often hundreds of replies, the manager may ask other senior members of his staff to assist. Clearly, this task is to be done as quickly as possible, not only for the sake of the applicants, but also because allocation of staff costs the firm quite a lot of money.

The setting up of interviews requires an appropriate room, with an adjacent waiting room; either an individual interviewer or a panel of interviewers; the organisation of any practical tests (such as in shorthand, typing, use of office machinery, etc.); and, of course, the notification to both successful and unsuccessful candidates, after the final interviews. (Often there is more than one interview.)

9.2   The Applicant

Presentation is very important when applying for a post and you should consider very carefully what impression you are going to create. Two areas in particular require thought and preparation:
  (a) the letter of application
  (b) the interview.
Before we look at these, however, there are some important questions that require an honest answer. How suitable do *you* think you are for the post for which you are applying? If you get it, will you be capable of doing it, once you have 'learned the ropes'? Have you a *real interest* in the type of work you are asking for, or do you think you will find it boring after a while? In other words, does it seem to offer *job satisfaction* as well as money?

How will you cope with working with a variety of people, some of whom will be much older than you; some of whom may not seem to like you, and some of whom you may dislike, but will have to work with? How *high* will the *standards* you set yourself be when you are given a job to do? Can you take criticism, and put up with 'being told off' if you make a mess of something? Will you be a *loyal* worker or will you be interested only in yourself and how little you can 'get away with'?

All these, and similar questions, can be summed up as *self assessment*. You may be asked to attend an interview where you expect to be 'assessed', but before you even apply for the post, you need to think carefully about yourself and what you intend your attitudes to be, to the work, to other people and to the 'bosses'.

To apply for a post just for the sake of having a job may be a great temptation, but could be a disaster!

If we suppose you have faced these questions honestly, and still decide to apply, then quite probably you will have to get an application form or write a letter of application.

The application form

This varies in content from firm to firm, but basically it will ask for whatever information the prospective employer requires. It will probably consist of something like this, following the firm's usual heading:

(a) The TITLE of the post advertised

(b) PERSONAL DETAILS (name, address, telephone number, age, sex, date of birth, nationality, married status, number of dependent children, medical history, etc.)

(c) EDUCATION (schools, colleges attended with dates, qualifications, technical or professional training, knowledge of foreign languages, etc.)

(d) EMPLOYMENT HISTORY (what experience, kinds of job, names and addresses of previous employers, position and duties in firm, salary you received, reasons for leaving, etc.)

(e) OUTSIDE INTERESTS and HOBBIES (any community work, sport, music, drama, etc.)

(f) ANY OTHER COMMENTS you wish to make

(g) SIGNATURE and DATE.

This form needs to be read and thought about *carefully* before being filled in *neatly* and *clearly,* in ink.

The letter of application

The first thing to have in mind if you write a letter of application is that it will give your prospective employer his *first impression* of you and we all know that when we meet someone for the first time, even if it is only through a letter, we form an opinion about them, for better or for worse. Of course, it is equally true that that opinion may be modified or changed when we get to know the person better. However, if a letter of application is poorly presented there will be no further opportunity for the prospective employer to get to know you, as the very appearance of the letter and the way it has been written will close the door to any future contact.

Appearance is important. Clean, unlined paper should be used, and the letter should be either handwritten or typed. Some employers prefer a handwritten letter, as it gives them an

introduction to your handwriting. If you are a typist, however, and
have access to a machine, a well-presented *typed* letter could help
towards supporting your application for a post involving typing.
But, the typing must be *accurate*! And that means, no overtyping,
no frequent use of correcting fluid, and certainly no grammatical,
spelling, or similar errors in the text!

The pattern or layout of your letter should follow the pattern of
the application form, indicated above. Neither make the letter too
long (a page to a page and a half of A4 is probably about right) nor
omit any details that may improve your chances of getting an
interview. After all, the employer will know only as much or as
little as you tell him.

The letter needs to be thought about carefully, and it is probably
best to write out a rough draft or two before attempting the final
copy.

Let us look at the kind of letter that follows the pattern of the
application form, as suggested:

```
                                          12 Pottery Lane
                                          CROXBY

                                          (date)

(Name and address of firm,
 as given in the advertisement)

Dear Sir

Post of Secretary to Sales Manager

With regard to the above post, advertised in yesterday's 'Croxby Clarion',
I would be grateful if you would consider this application, as I believe
I have the necessary qualifications and experience required.

As an Application Form is not asked for, the following details may be
helpful:

(1)  I am 20 years of age, and for the past three years have been employed
     by H Rankin & Co as general typist with a fairly wide range of
     responsibilities.  These include opening and distributing the morning
     mail; maintaining the filing system; typing letters, accounts etc,
     using the photocopier and other office machines; keeping the general
     office accounts; manning the switchboard, and acting as a receptionist
     from time to time.

(2)  I was educated at St Hilary's Comprehensive School, and gained 'O'
     level certificates in English Language and Maths (grades B and C) and
     several CSE certificates including Geography, Typing, and Oral English.
     I then attended a full-time Secretarial Course at Croxby Technical
     College, and gained the LCC certificate in Secretarial Studies,
     together with RSA Shorthand (100 wpm), Typing (45 wpm), Office Practice,
     and Accounting - both Grade 2.  This year I am studying for the Private
     Secretary's Certificate as a part-time student, for which my employer
     kindly arranged day-release.
```

(3)   My leisure time is well filled, as I am a member of a Swimming Club,
      and the Amateur Dramatic Society. I am also interested in dancing,
      reading, and needlework. I live at home with my widowed mother, so
      have few domestic responsibilities, which means I should be available
      for evening work occasionally, or to work late if required.

(4)   Although I am happy in my present employment, and get on well with
      my colleagues and senior staff, the post you advertise would be a
      promotion, and offers opportunity for PA work, in which I am
      particularly interested.

      My present salary is £XXXX. No doubt this is a matter which might
      be discussed should you grant me an interview.

(5)   My general health is very good and I have no disabilities. I have
      had no time off for illness in the past three years, and I believe
      that my punctuality is excellent.

(6)   The following have kindly agreed to supply references if required:

      G D Scholes Esq, H Rankin & Co, 173 Westgate, Croxby.
      (Present employer)

      Frank Pendleton, Producer, Croxby Amateur Dramatic Society,
      Theatre Royal, Croxby.

      J Hopper Esq, BA BCom, Head of Department of Business Studies,
      Croxby Technical College, Fairfield Road, Croxby.

As I am very interested in the post advertised, I hope that you may
invite me for an interview, when I can supply any further details you
may require. During office hours, my telephone number is Croxby 4371, and
my home telephone is Croxby 2224.

Yours faithfully

Perhaps at this point we should look at the paragraph on general
health, because it raises a question. If you have a relatively minor
disability, say very slight diabetes or epilepsy that is well under
control, should you mention it? The general opinion seems to be
that you should, either on the application form or in any letter of
application. To say nothing until the interview, or, worse still, to
wait for the matter to be discovered after you have been appointed,
may well mar your future relationship with the firm.

Reasons for wanting to leave your present employment can
present a difficulty too. For example, it would be very unwise to
say that you wanted to leave because you could not get on with
someone on the staff. Equally, it would be unwise to say you
wanted to leave because the working conditions were uncomfortable, or that your wage or salary was poor, or that you
sometimes had to work late which interfered with your social life.
On the other hand it would be quite reasonable to say that you saw
no likelihood of promotion or that you wanted a post with more
responsibility; but try not to sound complaining or disgruntled.

Prospective employers are not likely to be impressed by anyone who seems to grumble.

If you are asked on an application form or in an advertisement to state what salary you would expect, it is best to be cautious. If this is your first job you are not likely to be asked, but if you are, it might be best simply to say you would be glad to discuss the question of wages or salary at an inverview, should you be given one. If you are already working, state your present salary, and again, leave it open for discussion, as in the sample letter given above.

References and testimonials

There seems to be considerable confusion in the minds of some as to what a *reference* really is, and more particularly, how it reaches the prospective employer.

No reference is actually given *to* the person applying for a post. All the applicant can do is send the name and address of a possible referee to the prospective employer, who may then ask the person or persons named for the reference, which is forwarded *directly to the prospective employer*. In other words, *you,* the applicant, *do not see* the reference at all.

A printed form may be sent for a reference; this is because not every prospective employer wants a general reference. Some employers such as the National Health Service, banks, etc. require references that answer 'specialist' questions regarding the fitness or otherwise of the applicant for their posts. For example, the qualities required of a nurse are different from those required of a copy-typist; handling money and confidential matters is an occupation requiring certain qualities that are not so essential in other occupations. So by using a printed reference form, the prospective employer can ask the particular questions, in relation to the post applied for, to which he needs answers.

When sending a letter of application, it is a good idea to name three *kinds* of referee if possible: one who can write about your *work,* one who can comment on your *character,* and one who knows you *socially,* through your interests and hobbies, particularly if she or he knows you through any group activities.

Do remember, however,. that you should *not* give a name and address of a referee unless you have first asked the person's permission.

Some companies have now abandoned the use of references, though at one time references were regarded as essential. Other employers, such as the Civil Service, Government departments, banks and building societies, hospitals, schools, and most organisations within the public sector, will almost certainly require references. So if you are thinking of work in these areas, you must have your referees in mind before you make an application.

Almost anyone can be asked to be a referee for you, but obviously, the more 'established' a referee is, either professionally or in business, the more impressed the prospective employer will be. You should not ask relatives to be referees, of course, as they would be considered to be biased in your favour, but otherwise there are few restrictions on whom you can ask. One good guide is the list of people considered to be 'qualified' to support your application given on passport application forms. Although there are no regulations governing your choice of referees to support your application for a job, you may find the 'official list' in passport regulations helpful.

Testimonials are different from references in several ways. In the first place, they are written and *given to you* by someone you have asked. You may send copies with an application letter. Prospective employers, however, tend to take little notice of testimonials.

A curriculum vitae

A curriculum vitae (CV) is a 'history of employment' with additional details. It is usually set out as a kind of table, as shown in the example on page 117.

As you can see the outline lists all previous jobs. Should there be any gaps between jobs these should be explained—perhaps there was a period of unemployment or a period in hospital. Whatever the cause, it should be stated so that your 'history' is complete.

Clearly, the sending of a CV to a prospective employer will cut out much of what you put into a letter of application. This has certain advantages:

(a) for the prospective employer in that he can see at a glance how you have spent your years up till now;

(b) for you, as once your CV is carefully prepared it can be photocopied as many times as required for the number of applications you may have to make before securing an appointment to a post.

It may be worth noting that no letter of application should be copied. You should always send a top copy to any prospective employer, though you may retain a carbon copy or photocopy for your own records. Copied CVs, on the other hand, are perfectly acceptable to a prospective employer.

CVs take a considerable amount of time and thought to compile accurately and completely but need only be up-dated when the details on them change.

```
                    CURRICULUM VITAE

Name:
Address:
Tel:
Date of Birth:
Marital Status:
Nationality:

Education:
Schools and colleges attended (give dates in years)

Qualifications:
(give examination results, and dates in years)

Previous Employment:
Employer: (give name and address)
  Dates of service:
  Position held: (e.g. office junior, clerk)
  Main duties: (give details)

Employer:
  Dates of service:
  Position held:
  Main duties:

Employer:
  Dates of service:
  Position held:
  Main duties:

Interests: (give details of outside work activities)

Other: (e.g. do you have a clean driving licence?)

References: (give names and addresses of referees)
```

9.3 Preparing for an Interview

Again, this is a matter of *presentation*. There are several factors that will either enhance or detract from your presentation of yourself, which is what an interview is all about.

Appearance
The prospective employer wants to know as much as possible about you, but his first impression (other than the one created by your

letter of application or CV) is your appearance. Of course, it depends very much on the kind of job you have applied for. A manual worker, such as a garage mechanic or builder's labourer may dress in a fairly casual manner, but a prospective employee in an office needs to be a little more thoughtful. For example, it is *not* a good idea to appear in jeans or jewellery however frequently you wear these socially. Neatness and tidiness are really the key words. Try neither to overdress nor to be too casual and you are more likely to create a good impression. Bear in mind that you will be expected to maintain a neat appearance if you get the job!

Speech
This is also important. As an employee you will probably have to communicate verbally with a lot of people. A prospective employer will be assessing how well you can express yourself, how you might relate to customers and clients, how you might sound on the telephone, as well as how well you answer his or her questions. *Think* before you speak, and do not be afraid of pausing to think before giving an answer. A good interviewer will not expect you to have answers on the tip of your tongue, and will be much more impressed if you show that you are thinking as well as simply talking.

Answering questions gives you an opportunity to tell the employer about yourself. Avoid 'yes' and 'no' answers (in any case, a good interviewer will avoid questions that require just these replies), and try to enlarge and develop the answer you give to reveal as much of yourself and your thinking as possible.

Look at the questioner as much as possible. Perhaps when thinking, you may look elsewhere, but when speaking, try to speak *to* the questioner, not to a corner of the room or to your feet!

Listen to the questions. Try not to let anything distract you. If you are before a panel of interviewers, look at the one who is questioning you at the time, but when replying, try to look around the panel so they all feel included in the reply.

Usually, you are given the opportunity to ask questions yourself. Have them *prepared* beforehand! And *do not* start with questions about holidays and pay! Ask these later on, if they have not been explained, but avoid giving the impression that these are the most important things in your life! The opportunities for further training, the possibilities of late working or overtime, whom you are answerable to—all these are areas to think about *before* the interview, so that you are well prepared.

Do not be afraid to *smile* from time to time. But, on the other hand, however light-hearted and witty the interviewer may be, do not try to be funny in your replies. Show that you take the situation seriously.

One of the most difficult questions to answer, and one that is often asked, is: 'Why do you want this job?' This gives you the opportunity to show your interest in the firm. If you have done your homework properly you will have found out what the firm does and something about the range of its activities. Try to say what you think *you* can contribute towards those activities. It is not easy, but it is well worth a try, and shows at least that you have taken the trouble to find something out on your own initiative.

Nerves

Perhaps the greatest problem, when going for an interview, especially for the first time, is nerves.

Firstly, we must remember that this is perfectly natural, and that the interviewer is probably well aware of it—in fact, the interviewer may also be feeling nervous!

Secondly, take a deep breath or two before you enter the room. This will help to steady you. A piece of gum or a sweet just *before* the interview will ease the dryness of your mouth (but *do not* go in chewing). Try to sit in as comfortable and relaxed a manner as possible in the chair you are offered (but *do not* sprawl) and try not to perch on the edge. Knowing what to do with your hands is a problem for some. Why not simply clasp them in front of you on your lap? Occasionally you may need them to assist your speech but then return them to the clasped position.

A good interviewer will always try to put you at your ease and, since he has probably been through the experience of being interviewed many times himself, will know something of what you are feeling, so *stay calm!* Remember that you are there simply to give as much information as you can to help the prospective employer to recognise your potential, so say as much as you can (without being *too* talkative) in reply to the questions. Above all do not try to put on an act, just be yourself!

9.4 A Letter of Resignation

If you are given a position in a different firm and you are already employed, it is a courteous gesture to write a brief letter of resignation to the firm you are leaving. It should be addressed to your boss and may say, for example, that you have enjoyed working with the firm, but that the new opportunity gives you a chance of promotion; that you wish the firm you are leaving well in the future, and that you are grateful for all the help you have been given and the many friendships you have made.

Such a letter is not essential, but it is a gesture that many employers will appreciate. An example of such a letter is as follows:

```
                                                    Address

                                                    Date


The Personnel Manager
H Rankin & Co Ltd
173 Westgate
CROXBY

Dear Mr Scholes

In many ways I am sorry to have to be leaving the firm which gave me my
first job, but I have been fortunate enough to be appointed to a post
carrying much more responsibility and which is a promotion from the
position I held with Rankin & Co.

However, I would like to thank you personally, and the other members
of the staff for three years of great kindness and consideration, in
which I think I have learned a great deal.  I am also very grateful that
you agreed to act as referee if my new firm cared to take up the references.

I hope to be able to keep in touch with you all from time to time, and I
hope for the continuing success and prosperity of the firm to which I owe
so much.

Yours sincerely
```

A similar letter of thanks to your referees is not essential but will also be appreciated. There are no substitutes for considerate gestures such as this. It takes time and effort to *be thoughtful,* and some would regard it as quite unnecessary. Nevertheless, as this book has tried to point out, consideration is the key to good communication, in business as well as at home. As a reader or listener you should give of your full attention and try to empathise with the other person; as a speaker or writer you should express yourself clearly, logically and grammatically, without prejudice, but with judgment and good manners.

If you remember, also, that presentation is something that is important every day, not just on the day you apply for a job, then you will not go far wrong in your chosen career.

Assignment

Instead of the usual Questions, you are invited to consider the following assignment, which contains elements of many of the preceding chapters. This is based on a work situation, and provides an opportunity to practise some of the skills that by now you should have acquired.

The following advertisement appears in your local paper:

> Vacancy for an office worker in the Silverstream Travel Agency. Duties involve dealing with clients wishing to book holidays, using a computer, filling in forms, and making all arrangements on behalf of customers. Previous experience is not necessary; training will be given. Keen and enthusiastic applicants should apply by letter to: Silverstream Travel Agency, 43 Exeter Road, Croxby, by October 1st. Starting salary is £XXXX p.a. with good prospects of promotion. Hours are from 9–5 p.m. with occasional late-night work when required.

1 Write the *letter of application* for this post.

Your letter of application results in your being invited for interview.

2 Prepare *four questions* that you would ask, if given the opportunity, at the interview.

You have been appointed to the post, and have now been working for the firm for over a year. Because of your enthusiasm and conscientious work, you have been promoted to a higher grade of responsibility.

One morning you find the following letter on your desk:

```
Dear Sirs

My wife and two children and I have just returned from one of the most
harrowing experiences of our lives. We booked a fortnight's holiday in
Tangier through your Agency, and have had nothing but trouble and
frustration.

First, the flight was delayed by three hours, after which, when we
landed at the airport, we found that there was no-one to meet us, and
that one of our bags was missing. After two hours of waiting, the bag
was finally discovered, but it was damaged and had obviously been opened.

When we arrived at the hotel, the San Georgio, just outside Tangier
(having had to pay an exorbitant charge for a taxi), we were shown to a
```

room which appalled us. The floors were bare, apart from one small
rug; there was a strong smell of cooking in which boiled cabbage seemed
to predominate, and we found there was only one bathroom and lavatory
on our floor for us and some twenty other visitors.

We asked to change the room but were told that there were no other
vacancies.

While the food was reasonable, the service was very very slow, and after
two days both my wife and I suffered from a 'tummy-bug' which meant
frequent visits to the toilet, where we discovered to our horror and
great discomfort we often had to queue!

At night we could hardly sleep for the noise made by taxi drivers shouting
to one another, sounding their horns, and generally making a din until the
very early hours of the morning.

After a week of this, we approached the courier and asked if we could
return home. We were told that as we had booked for two weeks, according
to our agreement, no flight could be arranged and we would have to wait
until our return flight the following week. We waited, and have now,
thankfully, returned home. But this disastrous holiday has cost me over
£1000 and I feel that your company should return at least the cost of the
hotel as some recompense for the discomfort we endured.

Unless you make some reasonable offer, I shall be compelled to put this
into the hands of my solicitor.

Yours faithfully

Ivor Payne

3 Write a *memo* to your managing director about this letter,
   summarising its contents and asking for instructions.

You receive a memo from the managing director saying that the
company cannot accept any liability for the hotel but that enquiries
will be made to avoid any recurrence of this situation. The
managing director is going to fly to Tangier to make personal
enquiries, and you are to inform your branch office in Tangier of
his arrival at the end of the week.

4 Write a *letter* to Mr Payne telling him of the company's
   decision.
5 Send a *telex* to the branch office in Tangier informing them of
   the managing director's arrival. Their telex number is 007895
   Silstream. *Draft the telex message* (invent dates and times, etc.).

Meanwhile, a very different kind of letter has arrived on your
desk. It is as follows:

Me an the wife ave decided too give are daugter a wedding present when
she gets wed next easter. We want to book an oliday for them as there
not going to get one. What ave you got for spain. Will you send us
some details, please, sose we can chose. What with him been out of work
we seen this as a grate chance for them to getaway for a few days. I
hope it wont be to dear.

yours Sincerly

Mr F Bloggs

6 *Re-write this letter* correcting any errors in spelling, grammar or
   construction. You may rephrase it if you think it necessary.